Brilliant ideas

Brilliant features xiii

Introduction xiv

1. **Who you are is what you get**...1
   To transform your life you have to understand how to take full responsibility for what you
   can make happen. And this means learning the difference between what you can control
   and what you can't.

2. **Are you two people?** 5
   Do you live life as though you are two people? Is there one person for work and another
   one for home? Or one for strangers and another for friends?

3. **Did someone say something?** 9
   If you better your communication skills you'll also improve your relationship, enhance your
   performance at work and create more enjoyment in your social life.

4. **The impact of appreciation**..13
   Everybody needs to know that they're appreciated. However, it's easy to forget this and
   simply criticise the performance of our team and the behaviour of our families and friends.

5. **Behind the image**..19
   Making assumptions about people from first impressions is at best unfair and at worst very
   dangerous. It can lead you to treat people as though your perception of them is true.

6. **Creating our own reality** 23
   A positive mental attitude can transform a glass from being half empty to being half full
   and then actually help to fill the glass.

7. **What do I think about me?** 27
   Beliefs can have both negative and positive effects on our lives. Recognising that a belief
   can be changed can be liberating and is the way forward to a more fulfilled life.

8. **I can do it – I can!**..31
   A common belief is that confidence is a cloak or a set of skills that can be acquired in
   order to become more effective. Moreover, we often let a supposed lack of confidence stop
   us from doing things that we want to do.

9. **How will they cope without you?** 37
   Leadership – at work, at play or with family – recognises different styles of approach to
   inspire individuals to act in the best interests of themselves and of the group.

10. **It's a team game** 41
    It's probably easier to live life to the full if we have people around us who support and
    encourage us.

11. **Who's pulling your strings?** 45
    Are you really making decisions for yourself? Or are there times when you feel out of
    control, as though you have no choices?

12. **What made you do that?** 49
    We can look at motivation from two perspectives: motivation that costs money and
    motivation that costs your time. Whether at work or at leisure, it's helpful to understand
    these different ways of motivating people.

13. **Do they ask for it?**...55
    If we assume people are workshy, untrustworthy and lack commitment and then proceed
    to treat them as though this is how they are, they'll probably start to exhibit this kind of
    behaviour.

14. **What comes first?**..59

We have many needs in life, and some won't even surface until others are truly satisfied.
To help others fulfil all their needs is a key role for a great leader.

15. **Whose idea is it anyway?** 63

Great teamwork is encouraging other people's ideas and then building on them. We
immediately have a supporter – the person whose idea it was! We may also end up with an
even better idea.

16. **Please, let me think!** 67

Think things through properly and you'll make better decisions. Moreover, helping others
to think things through will improve their decisions and at the same time enhance your
leadership and relationship skills.

17. **Encourage to inspire**..73

The motivation to change has to come from within us. People can, of course, encourage
us in a number of ways, but ultimately motivation isn't an external energy.

18. **Liberate your thinking**..77

Many people believe that there are barriers limiting their ability to succeed or achieve
their maximum potential. These barriers need to be removed in order to allow a different
and clearer way of thinking.

19. **Boost your thinking power** 81

It's exciting and liberating to think beyond our self-imposed limits. Above all, it gives us
the opportunity to make a real difference in our own lives and the lives of others.

20. **Don't live your life by accident**..85

We do have a choice about how we live our lives. For example, we can choose to focus
on work. Alternatively, we can place a higher priority on family and leisure. Whatever our
choice, how do we get the balance just right?

21. **It's your choice** 91
    We live the lives we choose to live. We react to people the way we choose to react to people. However, what we believe about ourselves can limit our choices and make us feel like victims of circumstance or mistreatment.

22. **Who is in charge of your life?** 95
    It's too easy to live your life the way others want you to live it. Even scarier, you may not even recognise that you're doing it.

23. **Talk in their terms** 99
    We spend a lot of time communicating with people in the hope that we'll be able to influence them in some way. We know the outcome we're seeking and the action we'd like them to take. Here's a way to maximise your ability to influence people.

24. **Why plan your life?** 103
    I spent most of my life believing that I was doing what I wanted with my life. Then I realised that I wasn't my own person at all as I'd never actually sat down and thought hard about how I really wanted my life to be.

25. **When feelings hamper thinking** 109
    How many times when you've been furious or deeply upset have you said or done something that you bitterly regret? I bet you still squirm when you think about these moments.

26. **Am I hearing you?** 113
    When helping others to come up with ideas and make their own decisions, use their language not your's. It's extraordinary the influence you can have just by listening to people and even by simply getting them to repeat what they've said.

27. **Tell me how I'm doing** 117
If we truly want to become the best we can be – in any field of endeavour – then we
need someone who can tell us, openly and honestly, how we're doing.

28. **Do I have that right?** 121
Good communication enhances relationships. The mood of a family dinner or the success
of a business meeting can be transformed when we actually understand each other rather
than simply think that we do.

29. **But I asked you to listen to me** 125
When someone's thinking hard in order to reach the best decision about something,
we can fall into a trap called 'giving advice'. This often hampers the thinker and can be
devastating.

30. **Young people can think like giants too** 131
When it comes to imagination, experience can be a handicap. As we grow older, our
thinking can become increasingly restricted, preferring traditional thoughts to imaginative
ones that could transform our lives.

31. **What will become of us?** 135
In a relationship, life is apt to take over and we can begin to drift apart without
realising that it's happening. Suddenly we can find that we don't actually know each other
any more.

32. **Your moment of choice** 139
Your moment of choice lies in the gap between stimulus and response. Taking
responsibility is the most empowering thing you can do once you truly understand its
meaning.

33. **Appreciating diversity** 143

Appreciating a diversity of views and ideas can encourage us to let go of some of our limitations and enable us to think more deeply.

34. **Thinking quality? Think equally** 147

We think best when we're with people we feel comfortable with. Feeling 'inferior to' or 'better than' someone limits this ability.

35. **We are what we decide to be** 153

Three kinds of assumptions can hinder changes we wish to make in order to achieve the life we want and deserve: facts, possible facts and bedrock assumptions. We can think our way round all of them.

36. **Learning from mistakes** 157

We can choose to either learn from our mistakes when they happen or believe that we're just unlucky and go on to repeat the same errors.

37. **What else do I think about me?** 161

Your beliefs about the roles that you are to play in life can lead you to places you really don't want to be.

38. **Love is a choice** 165

When we fall head over heels in love it's easy to believe that this wonderful, euphoric feeling will last forever. As everyday life takes over, however, this feeling gets pushed aside.

39. **Be careful how you say it** 169

Communication isn't as easy as we might think as words mean different things to different people. When we want to disagree with someone we need to focus on the outcome that we'd ideally like.

40. **Laughter is the best medicine** 175
    We choose how we think and don't have to be driven by our emotions.
    Recognising that we can choose to be happy whenever we want is unbelievably
    empowering.

41. **Every day counts** 179
    Every day we're presented with the opportunity to have a new beginning and say,
    'Today I can choose how I think and feel in each and every moment.'

42. **Are we all leaders?** 183
    Whatever the role – boss, friend, parent or colleague – the minute that you're in a
    position where you can influence another person you are, in fact, leading.

43. **How we view the world** 187
    External influences condition our thinking and create subconscious beliefs that can
    affect how we react to people and situations. We need to be aware of our conditioning and
    beliefs in order to achieve top-quality thinking.

44. **How do I persuade them?** 193
    We all want to steer people towards our way of thinking. So, what's the most effective
    way of influencing people?

45. **No more indecision** 197
    We don't often ask ourselves who we really want to be. Yet, this is fundamental to
    how we live our lives.

46. **No, no and no** 201
    Learning to say 'no' in an acceptable way, without being defiant, is a skill that we
    really need to develop.

47. **Egg timer peace** 205
Developing an understanding of another person's viewpoint is the first step to resolving
issues between you and other people.

48. **A problem or an opportunity?** 211
How we view problems can make a big difference. We can either turn them into
opportunities or into bigger problems.

49. **Involve them all** 215
Some people are quieter than others at meetings. They might be nervous about sharing
their ideas, and we need to find a way to help them.

50. **So where am I at?** 219
Trying to do everything at once can create a feeling of being overwhelmed. The ability
to focus on the key things can help you truly begin to transform your life.

51. **Living in the moment** 223
Far too much time is spent worrying about the future or the mistakes that we've
made in the past.

52. **Keeping it going** 227
I hope that you've adopted some new ideas and have a fresh vision for your life. You
can now continue along the exciting path of developing yourself to achieve everything you
wish for.

The end 232
Or is it a new beginning?

Acknowledgements 234

Where it's at 237
Index

Brilliant features

Each chapter of this book is designed to provide you with an inspirational idea that you can read quickly and put into practice straight away.

Throughout you'll find four features that will help you to get right to the heart of the idea:

- *Try another idea* If this idea looks like a life-changer then there's no time to lose. *Try another idea* will point you straight to a related tip to expand and enhance the first.

- *Here's an idea for you* Give it a go – right here, right now – and get an idea of how well you're doing so far.

- *Defining ideas* Words of wisdom from masters and mistresses of the art, plus some interesting hangers-on.

- *How did it go?* If at first you do succeed try to hide your amazement. If, on the other hand, you don't this is where you'll find a Q and A that highlights common problems and how to get over them.

Introduction

**Many of us can find ourselves feeling frustrated
with the way things are going at some point. We
can even feel total despair. Often we feel like
there's no way out of the situation, let alone any
hope of getting close to achieving our hopes and dreams.
Frequently we blame others or the circumstances for the way
we feel.**

I know this because this described me up until quite late in my life. But reading a
book that jolted my thinking was a catalyst. I discovered the way to totally
transform my life into a happy and exciting adventure, where I stretch myself and
my abilities to the limit on an almost daily basis. I only wish I'd done this sooner. In
this book I share my discoveries in the hope that they may help you to grasp the
opportunities that life presents.

PENNY'S ROAD

One day, at the age of forty-nine, I was walking my dogs in the woods and reflecting
on my life so far, which hadn't quite gone to plan!

I'd been abandoned at four months old by my mother and then packed off to
boarding school at the tender age of seven, where I was bullied, teased and very

lonely. My first experience of sex was when I was raped at the age of eighteen. I was engaged at nineteen and married by the time I was twenty. I had six children before I was thirty.

The trauma and abuse of three failed marriages had left me a total wreck, with no confidence and very low self-esteem. In addition, despite my father settling a small fortune on me just before my first marriage, with the help of my husbands I was now totally broke and facing a mountain of debt.

I had the added trauma of my second son having recently died. He'd been diagnosed schizophrenic at the age of eighteen and after an extremely challenging eight years suffered a heart attack at the age of twenty-six.

TIMELY INSPIRATION

To add to all this, my health was suffering and I had a chronic back problem. It was actually during a trip to see my osteopath that a book I discovered inspired me to really look at myself in a different way. This, along with a number of other books and a series of personal development workshops, started the creation of a new wave of thinking for me.

That day, right there in the woods with my dogs, I made my 'commitment to the universe'. I wasn't going to waste the rest of my life in the same way. It was time to recognise that the only common denominator in my three unhappy marriages was me. This meant one thing: any change had to start with me. In that moment I committed to change my thinking and create a new life and to become a success in my own terms and by my own efforts.

AND NOW

Now I'm sixty-one and thousands of people have changed their personal and working lives after understanding how I turned my life around. How the picture has changed!

I've been inspired so much by my family. I have a close, loving and mutually supportive relationship with my children and recent grandchild, which I cherish. I have my dream home in Berkshire, set in an acre of beautiful gardens and woodland, which I share with a very special partner and my collection of four-legged friends.

I run a successful training and consultancy business, with twenty-five colleagues and associates in my team. I've received glowing testimonials for my work from people as diverse as chief constables, heads of industry in three continents, professionals, fathers, mothers and children.

Perhaps most remarkable of all is that my own self-esteem, self-reliance and confidence in my abilities as mentor, coach, trainer and inspirational public speaker have blossomed to fulfil my dreams.

I changed my thinking and I changed my life. I created a vision of how I wanted my life to be and I'm now living my dream. And still my dreams expand. There have been no lottery wins or major pieces of 'luck'. It's all come about because I changed my way of thinking – about me, about life, about relationships. Then I took total responsibility for the transformation. So, just open up your mind to what's possible and what you can achieve. I hope these 52 brilliant ideas help start you on your way, wherever you are right now.

1

Who you are is what you get

To transform your life you have to understand how to take full responsibility for what you can make happen. And this means learning the difference between what you can control and what you can't.

I've wasted a lot of my life trying to control the things over which I had no control and getting more and more stressed when I failed.

It was always important to me how people treated me and if they didn't treat me in that way I spent lots of time trying to get them to do so – I thought it was my right.

UNDERSTANDING THE DIFFERENCE

As a group exercise on my Personal Leadership Programme I ask people how they'd like to be treated by everyone they meet. Together we come up with a list that almost always includes things such as with respect, honestly, openly, kindly, as an equal, with integrity, as an individual, and so on. I then ask them, 'Can you make people treat you this way?' Of course, the answer is absolutely not. We might be able to influence them, but we certainly have no control over making them. How often in life do we spend time trying to get others to treat us in the way we think

Here's an idea for you... **Look for someone in your family or team at work who's not performing as you think they could. Think about what you could give them that would enable them to improve their performance. It may include things like truly listening to them to understand their needs, giving them some more information, supporting and encouraging their ideas more, giving them appreciation or developing their skills and knowledge.**

we deserve to be treated and getting upset when they don't? I certainly behaved this way, especially with my children. The reality is this. We have no control over 'get', we only have control over 'give'. So the conclusion that we come to is that if we want people to treat us in the ways that are important to us, then we in turn need to be respectful, honest, open, kind, treat others as equals, behave with integrity and show that we think each person is unique. This doesn't necessarily mean that they'll then treat us in the same way, but it's certainly going to make it more likely. The key here is recognising where you do have power and where you don't. You can't control the way people treat you and if you can't control it, then why spend lots of time worrying about it? The only place where you have power is in areas where you do have complete control.

MOTIVATION – WHOSE JOB IS IT?

How often at work do you hear managers questioning how they could motivate their teams more effectively? However, where does motivation come from? It comes from inside of you. So, how can anyone push a button that's inside of you. The knack of motivation is getting them to motivate themselves. If you believe your role is to motivate them and you do a really good job, what happens when you're not there? So turn your thinking the other way round. Instead of thinking about how you can get them to perform better, how can you get them to be more creative and how you can raise levels of awareness, think instead about what you can give them to enable them to perform better, what you can give them to enable them to become more creative, what you can give them to help raise their levels of performance.

For some key pointers check out IDEA 4, *Impact of appreciation*; IDEA 14, *What comes first*; IDEA 19, *Boost your thinking power*; and IDEA 11, *Who's pulling your strings*.

Try another idea...

There's a huge amount of research supporting the effectiveness of this approach, often known as 'servant leadership', and you'll find books and articles about this everywhere. The guru of servant leadership is Robert Greenleaf, and he believes that you should turn an organisation on its head so, for example, the CEO is at the bottom and his focus is on what he can give his directors to enable them to become more effective in every way. And the directors are thinking, 'What can we give to our direct reports?', and so on. At the 'top' the people at the coalface are totally focused on what they can give to their customers to enable an even more fulfilling and profitable relationship.

This works in exactly the same way in your home life. What is it that you can give your partner or your children to enable them to become happier, more loving and more fulfilled?

'From what we get, we can make a living; what we give, however, makes a life.'
ARTHUR ASHE

Defining idea...

3

Q **This is so simple! I can't believe I didn't think of it before. How quickly will people change once I start doing things differently?**

A *That depends on how long they've been managed the 'old' way! Share with them, openly and honestly, what you've just learned and ask them what you can give them to enable them to become more effective. That will encourage them to take more responsibility for themselves.*

Q **One of my children is a real lazy little git! Nothing seems to get him motivated. He just sits around listening to music or playing computer games. I'm at my wits' end. What do you suggest?**

A *Been there, got the T-shirt! Do you still cook for him, clean for him and do his washing? Do you also tell him that he's lazy and doesn't do anything to help, and generally whinge at him most of the time? I was like that when my children were younger. Firstly, look for things where you can tell him he's doing well. There must be something! Secondly, stop doing things for him. Tell him you now believe that he's intelligent enough to be able to do things for himself and that you trust him to do them. Finally, get him to do his vision for his life and then ask him daily, 'If you knew you could you do one thing today that will take you closer to where you want to be, what might you do?'*

2

Are you two people?

Do you live life as though you are two people? Is there one person for work and another one for home? Or one for strangers and another for friends?

When you are with your boss, do you behave as you would at home? Do you talk about your feelings and instincts or do you resort to facts and figures?

THE AWAKENING

I've been a consultant for many years – too many to own up to! Ten years ago, I stepped out of my job for a while. This was for two emotional reasons and one business one. The business reason was the most complex. For many years I had been a trainer, which involved considerable management training. As a company we were very successful but something that always concerned me was that no matter how great people said the training was, once they returned to work they seemed to forget most of what they had learned before they had begun to put it into practice. This was unacceptable to me and I decided that I wanted to get out of the business. It was at this point that my second son died, and soon after that I left my third husband. The following year was a difficult one. I gave myself time to heal and did many

Here's an idea for you...

Ask yourself whether you behave at work as you do at home. If you behave differently then ask yourself why. Which is the person that you are comfortable with and which is the person you want to be? It may be that you would like to include elements of both. Now ask yourself what is stopping you from becoming one person. Identify each side's strengths and plan how you can take those strengths into both situations.

things to keep me occupied. I qualified in massage, sports massage, aromatherapy and reflexology. I became a Reiki healer, an AuraSoma therapist and qualified in hypnotherapy. It was a busy year! I also went on some personal-development workshops, ranging from the very intense to the seriously wild and wacky, including Date with Destiny, Landmark Education and Mind Control. The thing that began to fascinate me was this. There were countless business people at these workshops, and I asked several how they applied what they were learning to their work lives. The response was usually, 'We don't. This is for me not for work.' This response challenged me because it meant people were deliberately choosing to be two people – the home person and the work person. I then began to question whether it was possible to link the two halves and take personal development into the business world in a truly pragmatic way that would be acceptable.

HEAD OR HEART?

I think it was at this point that I started to recognise what might be happening. At most management training programmes, trainers are appealing to people's heads. Trainers are getting people to think about the best ways to lead, inspire and motivate, and they give them all sorts of models that make this easier to understand. Consequently, when people finish the programme, all that they have learned makes sense and what they need to be doing seems obvious. However, as soon as they get back to work, life takes over. Urgent work has built up while they have been away and needs to be dealt with. When they do eventually get the opportunity to look back at all the good things they have learned, a considerable amount has been forgotten. Why? Because their hearts haven't been engaged. The training was aimed at head level. We should be asking the question 'What sort of leader do I want to *be*?' and not just 'What do I need to *do* to be a good leader?'

This was my turning point. My whole life and approach changed. I now only run programmes that affect the whole person, and everything learned can be used at both home and work.

Are you clear about your values? If you are two people then you could easily have two sets of values. Take a look at IDEA 45, *No more indecision.*

Try another idea...

Defining idea...

'*You cannot expect the world to change until you change yourself.*'
ROBERT MULLER, co-founder of the University of Peace, Costa Rica

How did it go?

Q **Ouch! This was like a sock between the eyes. I'm definitely two people. My male colleagues often describe me as a 'woman with balls'! If I show a softer side at work won't people take me for a ride? Especially as a woman in a man's world?**

A *This is a common belief but I think the exact opposite is true. Being a great leader isn't about telling people what to do. It's about inspiring them to find the way to do it for themselves, and I would suggest that this takes more caring than telling.*

Q **I try to be one person but I'm aware that I can be two. I sometimes get them confused. I often come home and start ordering my wife and children around as though they are my employees! How can I become one person without changing my style so completely that my staff and colleagues look at me as though I've lost the plot?**

A *First, recognise that you've no control over how people think, so let go of that. Second, choose what sort of leader – as a boss and as a husband and father – you really want to be and then write down the qualities that this sort of leader would demonstrate. Now go for it! Ask people for feedback along the way so you can see how well you're doing.*

3

Did someone say something?

If you better your communication skills you'll also improve your relationships, enhance your performance at work and create more enjoyment in your social life.

We're inclined to believe that the important thing in life is what we say, how we say it and what we contribute to a conversation. All of that's important, but the real skill in communicating is how well we listen.

LISTENING IS AN ART FORM

I used to find it virtually impossible to keep my mouth shut! Partly because I care passionately about people and I want to use the wisdom I've acquired from all my life experiences to help people. I was so excited that I hardly ever waited for people to finish their sentences before leaping in with my thoughts. Teaching personal leadership showed me that many people do the same thing, often for the best reasons in the world. When I finally truly learned about the power of listening, I was shocked beyond belief at how I'd continually interrupted others and not listened. I'd always thought that I was a good listener!

Here's an idea for you... **At your next meeting or family discussion, listen to people and don't interrupt. Observe what's happening. How much real listening is going on? What opportunities are being missed due to interruptions? How many people can't get a word in edgeways? Whose ideas are being driven through? Consider how useful this behaviour is and how you can share what you have learned. What changes can be made to achieve better outcomes? Remember that people asked to change their behaviour will need to see the benefits of doing so.**

It's crazy because we'd like to be sure that we're making the best decisions possible in all aspects of our lives. How can we possibly do this if we never let people finish their sentences? Unless we listen to people, we won't fully understand what they're saying. Often when we probably don't have the full picture we leap ahead and make a decision, and then spend an enormous amount of time sorting the problems we've helped to create.

I recently read an amazing magazine article discussing the space shuttles *Columbia* and *Challenger*. The overall conclusion was that the accidents should never have happened because there were people further down the organisation who realised what the problems were. However, nobody was listening to them.

THE YELLOW BRICK ROAD

Imagine that you're walking down a yellow brick road to get to a beautiful castle. You can't see the castle clearly because it's hidden by mist, but you know you really want to get there and explore it. While you're walking, you meet a large group of people who you think will pass either side of you. They don't. They knock you over, trample all over you and kick you. Once they've gone, you get up and start heading towards the castle again. Soon you meet two great friends. They're going off on another path and, after lots of chat, persuade you to go with them before you go to the castle. You enjoy your trip with them but then return to the path to where you wanted to go in the first place – the castle. Next, you meet someone who knows exactly where you're going and doesn't want you to go there. That

If you want to explore this further and really give someone the time to think through a problem or opportunity, then see IDEA 16, *Please let me think.*

Try another idea...

person becomes violent and eventually drags you off to somewhere else. In reality, if there had been some police officers standing around they may well have arrested some of those people for physical violence.

Now imagine this scenario. You're in a meeting and you have an idea that isn't totally clear but you want to share it nevertheless. However, every time you try to open your mouth you find that everyone else is so busy talking about their ideas that you can't get a word in edgeways. Or they want you to look at their ideas first. Or you're told that your idea can't be considered because a decision has already been made.

What is the difference between these two pictures? I would like to suggest that there isn't one. One is physical violence; the other is mental. Every time you interrupt someone else it is in fact mental violence.

'The reason we have two ears and only one mouth is that we may listen the more and talk the less.'
ZENO, Greek philosopher

Defining idea...

How did
it go?

Q **At a meeting of the local cricket club I simply observed as you suggested. Nobody really listened to anyone else and there were non-stop interruptions. This helped me to understand my frustration with the group – we make such slow progress and have great difficulty making decisions. I know it'll happen again next time. What can I do?**

A *Before the next meeting talk to some or all of the group about it. See if you can get at least one ally to support you in suggesting that the group really concentrates on listening. At the meeting explain the impact of interrupting and perhaps get everyone to point out when someone does it. Make it fun rather than criticising and you may be surprised at how much more effective and enjoyable the meeting is. Another way to avoid interrupting is to have an object such as a ball and only allow the person who is holding the ball to speak. And if someone with a bad case of verbal diarrhoea won't let the ball go, they'll learn fast because no one will pass the ball back to them!*

Q **I've worked hard at this with my team at work. We're now so conscious of interrupting that the conversation is riddled with people apologising when they do it. Does it always remain so artificial?**

A *No. Eventually the team will internalise its listening skills and the conversation will become less jerky. Listening is actually a 'learned' skill, and like anything we learn it takes time and practice to become more natural. So don't worry if this very conscious listening continues for a while, as it's far better than the alternative.*

4

The impact of appreciation

Everybody needs to know that they're appreciated. However, it's easy to forget this and simply criticise the performance of our team and the behaviour of our families and friends.

I came across a young lad who'd been expelled from school, had fallen in with a bad crowd, was smoking illegal substances and was generally behaving badly. His worried parents couldn't see how to change his behaviour.

CONCENTRATING ON WHAT HE *CAN* DO

The lad's mother especially was always saying things like, 'Why don't you have different friends? These ones aren't good.' 'You must work harder or you won't get the results you need.' 'Keep your room tidy.' 'No, you can't ride a motorbike as it's dangerous.' 'You must do your share of the housework.' She said these things because she loved him, but nothing ever changed. I persuaded the lad's father not to criticise his son at all for one month, but instead to notice the things that he did well. So, when the lad's bedroom looked marginally less of a tip than usual, his

Here's an idea for you...

Telephone someone who's important to you and tell them what you appreciate about them. When they ask why you called, don't muddy the water by having domestic arrangements to discuss. Just tell them that the only reason you called was to thank them for their strengths and the value that they bring to your life.

father thanked him for making it look nicer. When the lad happened to hang his coat up rather than drop it on the floor, his father noticed and thanked him. And when the lad chatted happily at a meal rather than sitting in sullen silence, his father told him what a joy he was. At any given opportunity, his father appreciated his son for who he was and what he did.

Imagine how that lad might have been feeling up until that point – worthless, just one big problem. Under those circumstances, how could he see any hope for a way out of his difficulties? The new approach produced dramatic results and, to cut a long story short, he's now doing extremely well.

AIM AT 80% APPRECIATION, 20% CRITICISM

When was the last time you told your partner that you love them and how much you appreciate their role in your life? How long is it since you pointed out to your children what they're doing well at school as opposed to what they're doing badly? And do you know who our worst enemy in this regard is? Us. It's said that an actor only remembers the member of the audience who didn't clap. We play a half decent round of golf and only remember the half that wasn't decent. If we do this to ourselves, how much more do we do it to others? When I ask people in companies what sort of feedback they get from their managers, they almost invariably start by saying that they're told when they're doing something wrong.

Can you remember a day when you woke up simply feeling good? About life, about yourself, about everything? When you feel like that, how do you perform? Everything goes well doesn't it? You handle the call to a difficult client better, that sale comes in more easily, you handle a sensitive conversation with a friend more effectively. So, if we know that we perform better when we feel good about ourselves, why do we then criticise people and expect them to be motivated to perform better? It really doesn't make sense.

A lack of self-appreciation prevents us from achieving our full potential. IDEA 18, _Liberate your thinking_, looks at how limiting assumptions hold us back.

Try another idea...

I'm not proud of it, but this is exactly what I used to do with my children. Because I cared. I loved them so much that I didn't want them to make the mistakes that I'd made. So, I kept telling them where they were getting it wrong because I wanted them to be better next time. Now my concentration is different. I don't run away from issues. Instead I help my children to focus on their strengths and on what they're getting right. And because I concentrate on their strengths, they display their strengths more and more. If you focus on people's strengths, including your own, your life could change beyond recognition.

'You can make more friends In two months by becoming more interested in other people than you can in two years by trying to get people interested in you.'
DALE CARNEGIE

Defining idea...

How did it go?

Q   **There's someone at work that I don't like, and she knows it. How do I give her appreciation without her suspecting that I'm flattering her for my own ends?**

A   *There must be something that you can appreciate about her behaviour or her performance at work. Thank her for that and, as long as you're sincere, she'll appreciate your words. Continue to look for ways of appreciation on a daily basis. It might not happen overnight, but if you express appreciation like this you might even come to like her.*

Q   **I'm a social worker, and my teenage daughter understands a lot of what I do. When I try to give her appreciation she tells me not to 'social work' her. Her behaviour isn't ideal at the moment, and I want to use appreciation of what she does well to correct her other behaviour. How should I approach this?**

A   *Make sure that you're using words that only a mother could use to her daughter. Tell her with real sincerity that you mean every word you're saying. It's interesting that your training has created unusual difficulties in bringing your children up, but I'm sure it's brought you and your children benefits too. My children also 'appreciate' each other and sometimes they joke that this is part of Mum's philosophy. However, deep down they still really love it and it brings them closer.*

16

5

Behind the image

Making assumptions about people from first impressions is at best unfair and at worst very dangerous. It can lead you to treat people as though your perception of them is true.

When we first meet a person, we probably meet a mask that may have been developed over years. We all create an image of ourselves that we are comfortable with.

Have you ever met someone who seems very aloof or even arrogant and you're sure you won't like them? You may even avoid them. Circumstances then change and you're forced to spend time with that person and as you get to know them a different picture emerges of a shy, caring and gentle individual, quite unlike the first impression you had of them. This example is common because shy people often put up such a mask, keep their distance and rarely open up and show who they truly are. And if you don't give them the opportunity they may never open up, and you're likely to treat them in a way that's consistent with your first view. We must miss many opportunities, as we probably do this with each person we meet.

Here's an idea for you...

Next time you meet someone for the first time, see how quickly you can get beyond their mask. Ask questions that encourage them to share information that would usually take a long time to elicit. What are they passionate about? What things do they feel best about in their lives? What would they do if they won the lottery? Get them to talk about how they're developing themselves or what areas they're striving to make progress in. It'll be far more interesting than finding out what they do for a living, and the relationship won't stem from misunderstanding or prejudice.

MAKING ASSUMPTIONS BASED ON EXPERIENCE

Suppose someone from your childhood, perhaps a friend of your brother, treated you badly. He's tall, big and imposing. He bullies you, takes the mickey all the time and humiliates you in public. Not only that, but you see him doing the same to your friends and to the people he goes to school with. Flash forward now to a new boss who on the face of it shares some of that person's characteristics. Your boss is big and imposing and has a loud and forceful way of dealing with people. Whether you like it or not, there's a high probability that you'll use your previous experience and at an unconscious level believe that this person is also a bully. You may now act like you did with your brother's friend and be nervous around your boss, avoid him, not look at him when you speak, and so on. Sadly, this may not be who he is at all and he probably can't understand your behaviour around him. This can lead to lots of misunderstandings. If you can just encourage him to share some of his thoughts and ideas *before* you make any judgements, you may just be surprised and develop an entirely different relationship with your boss.

Remember that people make assumptions about you when they first meet you. Work on projecting an open and honest view of yourself each time you meet a new person. Just take the mask off. It takes courage but it's very valuable and allows you to form closer and more meaningful relationships quicker.

For further dangers of self-fulfilling prophecy see IDEA 6, *Creating our own reality.*

Try another idea...

GROUP INTRODUCTIONS

Group introductions are an important idea, especially with groups coming together for the first time. I invariably use two questions when I start one of my courses: 'Tell us a bit about you – the real you rather than just what you do.' and 'Tell us three things you feel really good about in your life.' There's always at least one person who amazes me with some aspect of their life and character when they are asked these questions. It probably challenges several perceptions I may have had. And when we talk about it as a group afterwards, the same is true for everyone. They've all got completely new insights into people whom they may have known for years and now realise they didn't know at all and, similarly, into people who they've only just met but who they'd already made judgements about. It's like the difference between seeing a Hell's Angel on his motorbike with all his gear and seeing the same person in the supermarket buying nappies for his baby. The first can appear threatening, yet the second is a picture of a caring Dad.

'Many a man's reputation would not know his character if they met on the street.'
ELBERT HUBBARD, US writer and editor

Defining idea...

How did it go?

Q **I asked a stranger at a dinner party what she felt good about in her life. I felt resistance and discomfort emanate from her. She then told me a few things that she seemed to be making up. Is this to be expected?**

A *Don't be put off, as people are generally very happy to talk about themselves to someone who's expressing genuine interest. However, some people aren't used to this, so I'd suggest creating a comfortable environment by being open about you first. In my training programmes I always start by introducing myself in a very open way. It almost gives the other people permission to do the same.*

Q **I've had a problem with the chair of a committee that I sit on. I told her that I was trying to develop my leadership skills and asked what she thought was most important about learning to be a leader. This was very useful in terms of getting beyond her mask, but it did reveal a major difference of opinion. How does that help?**

A *It helps very much, especially if you're intending to work with this person on an ongoing basis. Now you can open a dialogue where you share with her your views about leadership and then recognise the diversity that you have. You can learn to live and work with people with different values and principles only if you truly understand why they hold these views. Constructive diversity can be hugely powerful and can lead to the creation of new ideas from which both parties will gain.*

6

Creating our own reality

A positive mental attitude can transform a glass from being half empty to being half full and then actually help to fill the glass.

Your attitude towards the things you have to do makes the difference between getting the most out of them and seeing them as chores that are impossible to enjoy.

A SILLY STORY

Imagine there are two women who are both married to successful men. They live in the suburbs from where their husbands commute to the city every day. Their husbands come bursting in from work one day with the news that they've won the Salesperson of the Year Award. The reward is a week in San Francisco in a five-star hotel with a pool and all the luxury you can imagine. Not only that, but wives are invited.

Both men suggest that their wives head to town on a shopping spree to buy some new clothes, especially something stunning for the dinner and dance and gala presentation.

Here's an idea for you...

Choose a task that you're not looking forward to. Firstly, remember that whether or not you do the task is your choice. Now imagine having completed the task and how much you enjoyed doing it. Feel the pleasure of having completed it. Next set aside a time to do the task. Remember that you choose your thoughts,so it's down to you whether you feel depressed or energised about the task. If you feel depressed, the task will become more of a chore and the quality of the thinking you put into it will be reduced.

The first wife is excited and thinks, 'Brilliant, a day in town. I'll park in the car park, probably not too near the station because the commuters will have got there first, but it'll be safe and I won't need a taxi. I'll go up by train, which I love especially as I love people-watching. It's fun trying to work out what they all do by how they look and the newspapers they read. I'll also be able to have a nosey at people's gardens and see the different things they all do with the similar space. And when I get to the centre, there'll be millions of people of all different cultures and just the energy of the place will be exciting. Then I'll get a taxi and even though there'll probably be a queue, you never know who you'll get talking to and the cabbies are real characters. I might get some tips from them about where to go. Then I'll explore the shops, which I really enjoy. The challenge will be not to buy too much because I know there'll be so many things that I'll like. What fun, I can't wait.'

The second wife thinks, 'Oh no, I hate the city. I'll never find anywhere to park at the station because the commuters will have got there first. It'll probably be raining so I'll be wet and cold before I even get there. I probably won't get a seat and I bet no one will offer me their seat. Commuters are so boring, they just stare at their newspapers and ignore you. And when I get there, it'll be a nightmare with hundreds of people pushing and shoving. There's bound to be a long queue for a taxi and cabbies always take you the long way round and charge a fortune. Then I'll have to traipse round the shops. Shop after shop because I'll never find something I want, and the service is never as good in the big city stores. It's going to be awful but I suppose I'll have to go because I've got to find something to wear.'

Look at IDEA 32, *Your moment of choice*, to gain a deeper understanding of the meaning of responsibility.

Try another idea...

So, both women do go to the city. And what sort of day do they have? It's obvious isn't it – the first has a brilliant day and the second has an awful one. But just think about it – everything outside of themselves is identical, and yet they have a very different experience.

What you can say here is that these women created a day in their life by the way they were thinking. So, let's pause a minute and think about this because if we can create one day then perhaps we can create two days, a week, a month, a year or even a lifetime. This is actually amazingly exciting because it means that we have everything that we need to transform our lives. Change your thinking and you'll change your life.

'*Life is the movie you see through your own eyes. It makes little difference what's happening out there. It's how you take it that counts.*'
DENIS WAITLEY, trainer and motivator

Defining idea...

How did
it go?

Q **I have to attend a monthly meeting at work that's a waste of my time. It drags on, and most of the subjects are of no interest to me. I've plenty of better things I could be doing with my time, but my boss insists that I attend. What can I do about it?**

A *Firstly, it's your choice whether or not to attend the meeting, but if you wish to stay in your current job you may choose to go along. Most importantly, having decided to attend, you could choose to approach it thinking that you'll make the most of the time spent by communicating with and getting to know all of your colleagues better and contributing as much as you can. You may be surprised at how much the experience improves.*

Q **Whenever we visit my mother-in-law I have an awful time. The journey is long, she never seems to be very welcoming and I have to eat food that I'd never normally choose. I don't want to be impolite, so I have to put up with it don't I?**

A *No doubt it's important to your partner to see her mother. So, you may choose to adopt the approach that this is a way of showing your love and support to your partner. And if you decide to make the most of every visit and show that you're happy to be there, you may create a totally different experience. You could even offer to cook for her one day!*

7

What do I think about me?

Beliefs can have both negative and positive effects on our lives. Recognising that a belief can be changed can be liberating and is the way forward to a more fulfilled life.

Our upbringing and what we witness in our early years can dramatically effect how we live our lives. We can end up repeating useless patterns and believing that 'life has it in for us'.

WHAT WE DON'T WANT

Imagine you were born into this life as a pure spirit – a blank sheet of experience soaking up knowledge from the world around you. Say you're born into a family where the father is violent and, from a very young age, you hear raised voices and the noise of slaps and punches. You may actually see your father knocking your mother about. At a very young age you may begin to acquire the subconscious belief that all men are violent. And every time you hear or see your father hitting your mother or your older siblings it reinforces that belief. As this is your only experience of men, the unconscious belief may continue to develop.

27

Here's an idea for you... **Is there something holding you back from achieving something you've always wanted to achieve? Perhaps there's a subconscious belief that's stopping you. See if you can find it by asking yourself what you're assuming about this situation. Write down whatever responses come into your mind, however crazy they might seem. You may then choose to ask yourself a question along the lines of, 'If I could change my life to be exactly as I want it to be, what would I do differently, right now?'**

Now you've grown up a bit and go to school where you meet lots of lovely little boys – great kids who care about their friends and treat them kindly. But one day, in break time, you see two older boys bullying a younger child. Here's another reinforcement of your subconscious belief that men are violent. All the lovely boys you've seen count for almost nothing.

Later as a teenager you could be receiving abuse yourself – maybe physically, maybe sexually. Sadly, there's a real possibility that you'll assume that this is the way of the world. But as you grow older still, and spend time with friends and their families, you begin to realise that what you're experiencing isn't normality at all. Many of your friends have never been hit and neither have their mothers. You begin to realise that the pain you're going through is the exception not the norm.

SO LET'S CHANGE

At this point you may swear that the one thing you'll never do is treat your own children in this way. You'll be a very different person because you'll never allow children of yours to suffer in this way.

Look at the different level of beliefs or assumptions that we can acquire. The more we can bring them to our conscious awareness, the easier it becomes to move past them. Try IDEA 18, *Liberate your thinking.*

Try another idea...

The statistics on this are scary. According to current police evidence it appears that around 82% of abusers have been abused themselves. Crazy isn't it? At a conscious level, who'd ever want to put others through the pain that they themselves experienced? At a subconscious level, one can get some understanding of what's happening. In a much less dramatic way, and because of my early childhood experiences, I had the belief for years that I wasn't good enough. I kept trying to change the circumstances outside of me so that I could improve my life – I changed husbands, homes, ways of living, etc. It was a long time before I realised that nothing would change until I changed the belief itself. Another thing that appals me is something I learned recently. Research shows that about 80% of young offenders reoffend within two years. We keep trying to change them and give them new skills, a new environment, a new family. But perhaps we are working in the wrong area. Perhaps we need to help them to change their inner world and get them to explore the beliefs that may be holding them back from the change so desperately needed.

'The self is not something ready-made, but something in continuous formation through choice of action.'
JOHN DEWEY, US philosopher and educator

Defining idea...

29

How did it go?

Q **I don't hit my children, but I do lose my temper with them. I shout and scream and they run for cover. You could be right about a subconscious belief because my mother used to do the same, and I remember how much I hated it. Does this always happen?**

A *Not always, but pretty frequently in my experience. The first thing to do is bring the subconscious belief to your conscious awareness as you've already done. Then consider what you believe the role of a mother to be and how you'd like the relationship with your children to be. Consider the behaviours you'd like to see from you and them. Then take 100% responsibility for your behaviour and ask yourself whether shouting and screaming supports these ideals. How you behave is your choice. There's a gap between stimulus and response, and that's your moment of choice. Acknowledge that you're choosing to get angry, then consider what might be a more appropriate response. Once you truly acknowledge this, the anger will become much easier to deal with as you are in control.*

Q **My male boss shouts at us and uses heavy sarcasm to belittle us. I can handle it, but two of my female colleagues get very upset. How could I try and change him?**

A *We don't have control over changing others, only over changing ourselves. So what can you do differently to enable your boss to see that this behaviour is hindering rather than helping to achieve his objectives? Maybe on an occasion when he doesn't use sarcasm tell him how much more enjoyable you found the meeting and how much more productive it was. Perhaps share with your colleagues the thought that his behaviour is nothing to do with them, it is to do with him. Help them recognise that they could choose a different response and see what happens. If they consciously decide not to get upset, you may be pleasantly surprised at how your boss's behaviour may change in response. Remember that bullying only works if the person being bullied reacts to it.*

8

I can do it – I can!

A common belief is that confidence is a cloak or a set of skills that can be acquired in order to become more effective. Moreover, we often let a supposed lack of confidence stop us from doing things that we want to do.

I would like to suggest that this is a fallacy – an excuse as opposed to a valid reason.

TURN YOUR THINKING ON ITS HEAD

When I left my last husband, I was a mess. My confidence was so low that if I'd attended a workshop with a small group and been asked to speak, my voice would have been shaking, my hands would have been sweating, I would have been close to tears and I would have felt a fool. I also had a clear vision about what I wanted to do – help people to change their lives. The two didn't go together!

My eldest daughter asked me to give a talk to a small group, and I got myself in a state of panic. A friend offered to come down and support me and on the way there asked me how I was feeling about the talk. I told him I was in a complete panic, and when he asked me why I replied, 'I'll get it all wrong, forget my words, people will think it's awful, my voice will be shaking and I'll make a fool of myself.' I'll never forget his next words. He asked me, 'Why are you thinking about you?' I was

Here's an idea for you...

Think of a situation that you currently avoid as it makes you nervous, such as speaking your mind in front of colleagues or your boss, joining a club to meet new people or going to a party where you don't know anybody. Completely let go of how you feel about yourself and think about what you can give to others in this situation, such as giving your colleagues the courage to open up themselves, giving your boss a chance to understand you better or meeting a shy person at the party and showing him care and support. Promise yourself that you'll do one thing each week, however small, where previously you held back through lack of confidence and see how differently you begin to feel.

speechless for several minutes and then turned to him and thanked him. I realised in that moment that every time I had a confidence problem I was thinking about me. What would people think about me? Was I doing a good job? Did they like me and value what I was saying? I was focusing on what I could get, not on what I could give, when in fact I wasn't there to think about me. My life changed in that moment because I realised that I had absolutely no control over what other people thought about me. My reputation was outside of me, something I could do nothing about, so I could let go of worrying about it. All I had to do was speak from my heart, go out there and give all that I had to give and let go of the rest. Since then, I've spoken to over a thousand people and, although I still get butterflies sometimes, I'm aware that if panic hits I'm once again thinking about me. I entirely focus on what I can give and let go of the rest.

IT ONLY TAKES A MOMENT

Changing your thinking in this way can truly only take a moment. A young woman that attended one of my workshops was so nervous that her voice was shaking when she introduced herself at the beginning of the day and was still very wobbly by lunchtime. At the end of the day, I asked individuals to turn to the person next to them and tell them something that they really liked and appreciated about that person. I knew that this lovely young woman would really panic at the thought of doing this so I told her my story before asking her to do so. I suggested that all she did was look at the person next to her and really think about what could she say to the person that could make them feel good about themselves. I suggested she let go of everything else and forget there was anyone else in the room. She managed to do this brilliantly. Two weeks later she came back on day three of the programme. She was literally transformed. She is now one of my top trainers!

Look at IDEA 24, *Why plan your life?*, and consider creating a vision for your life that may include having the confidence to live it.

Try another idea...

Defining idea...

'Come to the edge, no we'll fall
Come to the edge, no we can't
Come to the edge, no we're afraid
And they came
And he pushed them
And they flew.'
GUILLAUME APOLLINAIRE

How did it go?

Q **I can hardly believe how powerful this is. At first I thought it was silly and that it couldn't possibly work, but I gave it a go. In a meeting I attended where normally I say nothing I really thought about what I could give. I realised how often people come out of the meeting unclear about what the boss has said. I realised I could help give this understanding to the rest of the team if I asked a question. I was nervous but I did it. Not only did it help the team, who told me so afterwards, but also my boss thanked me for asking the question. Is it always this powerful?**

A *Well done you! In my experience it is. When I truly let go of thinking about me then it works every time.*

Q **Do the awful feelings inside ever go?**

A *Every person is unique so I can't answer this. However, my experience is that the more you practise this, the more confident you'll become and the more the nerves will fade. There are still times when I feel the old panic rising and I just ask myself, 'Who am I thinking about right now?' It's invariably me. So I change my thoughts, which works every time. I find myself taking on tougher and tougher challenges and with each one my confidence grows. Just keep going!*

9

How will they cope without you?

Leadership – at work, at play or with family – recognises different styles of approach to inspire individuals to act in the best interests of themselves and of the group.

The full spectrum of leadership style starts with the autocratic and moves through five stages to the democratic. However, research has shown that the two more successful leadership styles – 'Push' and 'Pull' – comprise a combination of stages.

THE FULL SPECTRUM

At one end of the scale, the communicating style of an autocrat is 'Tell' – 'I want you to do this and this is the way that I want you to do it.' It's a very directional style that tells people what to do and probably every step of how to do it.
If the style moves slightly towards democracy it becomes 'Sells' – 'I want you to do this, but let me tell you why.' So, although still directional, people are given the reasons why the leader wants them to do it.

Here's an idea for you...

How do you behave when you're with your family? Do you tend to tell them what to do? Do you persuade them that your approach is the right one? Do you overpower them with your ideas? Next time a decision needs to be made, involve them all in the process – ask for their thoughts and ideas. Don't forget to support and appreciate their input.

If we move another stage nearer to democracy, we come to the 'Tests' style – asking for the opinion of the others involved. So it's still the leader's idea, only this time the leader's saying, 'This is what I think we should do and this is why, but tell me what you think.' The leader is now opening up to the team's ideas and modifications.

The next step is a 'Consults' style and this is when the leader may say, 'OK team, we've got a bit of a challenge or an opportunity here. Do you have any ideas as to how we might handle this?' This is the first time it's no longer the leader's idea.

The most democratic end of the spectrum involves the group taking on a challenge, deciding what needs to be done and then getting on with it with no direction from the 'boss'.

The 'Push' style of leadership is a combination of the first three stages, and the 'Pull' style is a combination of the last three, so they overlap in the middle.

WHICH STYLE GETS THE MOST CONTINUOUSLY SUCCESSFUL RESULTS?

Firstly let me say that there is no 'right' or 'wrong' here and that each is appropriate in certain circumstances. If the frying pan has caught fire we are not going to get everyone together to think of possible ideas for handling the situation. Let's face it; here it is appropriate to direct everyone for the safety of the family.

On the other hand, if you are constantly telling your team or your children what to do, how to behave and what you expect of them with no respect for their ideas or thoughts, you are unlikely to ever achieve long-term outstanding results. And this is aside from the fact that they probably will walk out of their job or become a totally rebellious teenager.

If you feel that you naturally tend to take a 'Push' approach and don't encourage others to develop their ideas, have a look at IDEA 39, *Be careful how you say it*.

Try another idea...

When most of us were growing up we were probably educated to believe that leadership was about being the one out in front telling everyone what to do. Asking everyone else what their ideas were was seen as 'weak' or 'soft'. However, the 'Pull' style, is now widely believed to be the strongest style of leadership there is. However, it is also the most challenging.

The most powerful form of leadership and the one that sustains outstanding performance is about involving everyone; asking for their view of the way ahead. This way, you are continually stretching people to improve. The 'Pull' style involves appreciating their contribution and recognising their achievements. Besides which, if you are trying to help everyone to develop and fulfil their potential, they need to think for themselves and be able to cope when you are not around.

'If you are planning for one year, plant rice. If you are planning for ten years, plant trees. If you are planning for 100 years, plant people.'
CHINESE PROVERB

Defining idea...

How did
it go?

**Q   It was a bit of a shock when I realised that I tend to use a 'Push'
style with my team. I want to change, but they seem reluctant to
come up with any ideas. It's as if they're not interested. Is it
worth pursuing?**

A   *Stick with it. It takes time to move from the 'Push' style to 'Pull'. Imagine
being in their shoes. If you'd never been asked for your ideas before and
always been told what to do, how would you feel when suddenly someone
asks what you think? Wouldn't you feel a bit nervous or suspicious? The
most important thing is to keep asking for their opinion and appreciating
their ideas, and eventually they'll start to believe that real change has
taken place.*

**Q   When we decided to discuss where we to go for our summer
holiday this year, our children suggested all sorts of different
types of holiday. Our discussion developed into an argument
because they all wanted to go with their choice. Was a discussion
a bad idea?**

A   *No. I think it's a good idea to involve the whole family in such a decision.
However, it may be a good idea to set some parameters next time. For
example, make the challenge to find a place that has something for
everybody, such as swimming for Joe, dancing for Jane, shopping for mum
and some historic architecture for dad. Suggest that they all go away and
think about it, and see what ideas they can come up with. Remember,
they've never had this level of involvement before, so perhaps they need a
little guidance.*

40

10

It's a team game

It's probably easier to live life to the full if we have people around us who support and encourage us.

We all know that teamwork is critical and yet for many of us it's a challenge. We often end up in competition with people rather than working with them.

THE FIRST TEAM

The first team that we become aware of in life is, of course, the family. When I was growing up, I don't think I ever realised this or thought of it in that way. Did my family work as a team? Only very rarely. I had an older brother and sister who were six and seven years older than me respectively and I must have been a complete nuisance to them virtually all the time. I wanted to be part of whatever they wanted to do, and they must have spent more time thinking up ways to get me out of the way than actually having fun. Dad was an amazing man and I totally adored him and can still clearly remember one thing that we occasionally used to do together where I felt important and part of his 'team'. He had a passion for fast cars,

Here's an idea for you... **Get your family together and draw up a vision for your ideal family – how it would be, how it would feel and what it would be doing. Discuss the strengths that each person might bring to this vision, the role each person would choose to play and the behaviour they may want to demonstrate. Now see how committed and determined each person is to creating that ideal. This process could be equally powerful at work with your team.**

and the older he got the faster they got. He used to take them for test drives, which included timing how fast they could go from 0 to 80 miles per hour. I was in charge of the stopwatch and, boy, did I feel proud. However, did we ever sit down as a family and think about how we could all effectively work and play together? Did we ever ask ourselves what our different strengths were and what we could bring to the family unit? Sadly, never. Even sadder is the fact that I didn't recognise how incredibly powerful this could be until after my own children had grown up and so I missed the opportunity to do it with them as well.

A DIFFERENT APPROACH

One of the things I discovered about myself in my period of huge growth following my many mistakes was that I didn't feel it was OK to ask for help. I thought that if I couldn't do it all for myself then I wasn't good enough. The other thing I discovered was that I was even less comfortable if I was in a position where I had to work with someone else. I really didn't like it if they wanted to do something differently to me. I wanted them to do it the same way as I would have done.

So, what's teamwork about? It's about knowing what you want to achieve, having a clear vision and then agreeing who has what strengths and abilities to bring to the party. Then each individual might think of all the ways that they could both do their bit and encourage and support everybody else to do theirs. Communication is critical to teamwork – ensuring that everyone knows how their bit is going so that any decisions that need to be made can be made with absolute certainty that all the necessary information is available. In my experience working in business, this is where it goes wrong nearly every time. Individuals can get so carried away with their part of the job that they forget what impact their decision could have on someone else's area, which can cause chaos and upset.

If you want to find out how the teamwork is going, get feedback from everyone. See IDEA 27, *Tell me how I am doing*.

Try another idea...

'The way a team plays as a whole determines its success. You may have the greatest bunch of individual stars in the world, but if they don't play together, the club won't be worth a dime.'
BABE RUTH

Defining idea...

How did it go?

Q **This sounded really formal and when I asked my family to do it their eyes rolled! Anyway, I got them all to sit down and after the rude comments had subsided we had a go. Everyone became quite excited and we came out with a really great vision and each made commitments to what we were going to do as part of this team. However, my husband was very dismissive afterwards and said it wouldn't work as the children would never stick to it. What can I do about his attitude?**

A *Your husband's attitude isn't very helpful and bearing in mind that our thinking creates our reality he could inadvertently sabotage the exercise. You'll simply need to provide even greater support in the short term and remain focused on the bits that are working. Tell the children how well they're doing and ask them how it feels to be part of a happy team. Keep letting your husband know how well they're doing, which will keep your spirits up and hopefully begin to change his negative attitude.*

Q **I find it easy to support and help others, but nearly impossible to ask for help for myself. How can I deal with this?**

A *This was always a problem for me too – I saw it as weakness if I needed help. However, think about how good you feel when someone asks you for help and how nice it is to know that you can do something to help someone else. We all like to be needed. Now ask yourself why you wouldn't want to give someone else the opportunity to feel like this. Think of it as giving something to others rather than taking something.*

11

Who's pulling your strings?

Are you really making decisions for yourself? Or are there times when you feel out of control, as though you have no choices?

If you're anything like me then there will have been many times when you've felt that everybody controls your life but you and that you're at everyone else's disposal.

WHOSE LIFE IS IT ANYWAY?

My life used to consist of nothing but 'should' or 'should not', 'must' or 'must not', 'ought to' or 'ought not to', and 'got to'. There was always someone telling me that I really *should* have written that letter before today, someone telling me that I really *must* get that work done today and someone else telling me that there was something that I really *ought* to do if I wanted to avoid this or that situation! Does any of this sound familiar? I felt as though my life was permanently under some other mysterious person's control, as though someone else was pulling my strings. I felt exhausted because there was always something else that I really *should* have done before I fell into bed. The silly thing was that I actually began to feel that I had no choice. Then I read a book that had a profound impact on both my thinking and my language. I realised that the language I was using to myself and others

Here's an idea for you... **Write disempowering words in big bold letters on Post-it notes. Draw big red crosses through them and then stick the Post-it notes where you can see them such as on the fridge, in your underwear drawer or on the edge of the TV. This will help you to realise how much you use these words and how little you feel in control. Change your words to 'choose to' and 'choose not to'.**

I had a client who wanted help dealing with his prostate cancer. When I asked him about his life he told me what he must and should be doing. He was putting control of his life outside of him – the prostate cancer was inside of him. I asked him to do the above exercise. He came back a week later having done very little different with his week, but he was very different in himself. Throughout the week he'd done everything by his choice. In changing his language he'd begun to take back control of his life. Now it was possible to begin to deal with the cancer.

wasn't helping in any way at all. I used those words to myself, and certainly others, virtually all the time and, consequently, felt permanently disempowered. I was putting the control outside of myself, and allowing myself to believe that I wasn't in control of my destiny. Not at all helpful. So, I changed my language.

SO WHAT DO WE CHANGE?

You may well say that language is semantics, and I would agree. However, does language have power? Certainly. Life has no meaning until you give it meaning. The way you describe something is likely to be the way it becomes. Say, for example, something happens and you say 'I'm absolutely livid'. What mood are you likely to create? Probably a feeling of being livid. If, however, you say that you're mildly irritated, then you're likely to feel exactly that – mildly irritated. So, language does have power.

Words such as 'should' and 'must' imply no choice and when we feel we have no choice, we can feel pressurised and consequently we don't think or perform as well. Instead use the words 'I choose to' or 'I choose not to', as the

More on being in control can be found in IDEA 22, *Who is in charge of your life?* It may be worth refreshing your thoughts.

Try another idea...

truth is that we always have a choice. We simply need to recognise that some choices are less comfortable than others. For example, when you say to yourself 'I really *should* get this work completed today' how do you feel when you think of this work and how well will you deliver? Now recognise that you have the choice whether or not to do the work today. Choosing not to may be painful – if you don't do the work you get the sack! But what about saying to yourself, 'I choose to get this work done today'? Now how do you feel about the work? Moreover, who is in control?

'*Language exerts hidden power, like a moon on the tides.*'
RITA MAE BROWN, US author and social activist

Defining idea...

How did it go?

Q **This sounded ridiculously simple, but when I started to really listen to myself I was amazed at how many times I used disempowering words – to my children. Does it affect the ones who hear it as much?**

A *In my opinion, yes. But ask them. How do you feel when you ask someone for advice and they tell you exactly what you really should be doing? Do you feel good? Or do you almost want to do something different for some reason? There is your answer. Think how you feel when someone says you 'should' or 'must' do something. Really make an effort to say things like, 'You have choices here, what do you think would be the most useful one for you?'*

Q **I began to listen to the language that my wife uses because I'm aware how resentful the children and I can feel when asked to do something. I realised that she uses disempowering words all the time. How can I change this?**

A *It sounds as though you think she's aware of the impact she's having and she may well not be. Why don't you suggest a really positive way that you might like her to ask you to do things and then respond to her requests very differently? Then suggest that she may like to do this with the children too because you're aware how much better you feel about doing things for her because of the way she now asks you.*

12

What made you do that?

We can look at motivation from two perspectives: motivation that costs money and motivation that costs your time. Whether at work or at leisure, it's helpful to understand these different ways of motivating people.

Motivation is encouraging someone to want to behave in a particular way or to really want to achieve something. It's an important element in handling our business and personal relationships.

THE EASIER ELEMENTS OF MOTIVATION

Imagine a young man who's just decided to go for a new job. At that stage he'll be thinking about the salary, the fringe benefits such as a pension plan or car, the location, what the office is like, the job title and status, the hours, the holidays and, of course, the job description.

Once he starts his new job, he'll start to look at things a little differently. The tangible things mentioned above, which we call hygiene factors, are unlikely to be the only source of motivation. In fact, they'll only ensure that a member of staff performs to the level required for the job and are unlikely to motivate someone to perform outstandingly. There's a heap of research that supports this view. For

Here's an idea for you... **Make a list of the non-hygiene factors that would motivate you at work, such as achievement, recognition, personal growth and responsibility. How many of these are present in your working environment? Now consider how you could motivate other people. What could you do differently tomorrow that might help your colleagues feel better about themselves and inspire them to perform outstandingly?**

example, we often think that the real motivator is money and it may be true that if you double someone's salary they will work longer and harder for a while. However, the research actually indicates that in fact it's no more than a few days before people go back to how they worked before, probably believing that they are well worth what they are being paid for doing the job.

Now this is not to say that these hygiene factors aren't important. Imagine that someone halved your salary. Just your salary, nobody else's. This will undoubtedly have a negative impact on your performance! So these factors form the basis for us taking a job in the first place and for performing to an acceptable level once we're actually at work.

OTHER MOTIVATORS

OK, so now we know that there's more to motivation than the tangible or hygiene factors. Recognition at work – perhaps for handling a situation well, achieving a production target or making a sale – is highly motivating. And all that this involves is taking the time to publicly thank and congratulate someone. Think of all the people who work in lowly paid but rewarding jobs, such as stable lads or charity workers. They care passionately about what they do and recognition is all the motivation they need.

It's the same with our families and other personal relationships. For example, we can give our children the best bedroom in the world with all the gadgets their friends have and more. Or we can make them the richest kids on the campus. But if we don't make the time to recognise their achievements, give them our heart-felt appreciation for their help and support or appreciate them just for being them, we put them into a sterile environment that ignores their emotional needs and wants and may well result in behaviour that we'd rather not experience!

IDEA 30, *Young people can think like giants too,* **might help you to involve your children in thinking about their interests.**

Try another idea...

'Celebrate what you want to see more of.'
TOM PETERS

Defining idea...

How did it go?

Q **I'm trying to help my teenage son to achieve better results at school. The problem is that he's simply not interested in any subject other than English. He reads a lot of novels but how do we motivate him to get on with other subjects?**

A *Most importantly, make sure that you really appreciate all of his efforts with English – tell him how well you think he's doing and how pleased you are. Then perhaps you could ask him what might encourage him to take a greater interest in other subjects. In other words, involve him. By continually praising his achievements in English, he may work harder to find ways to achieve in other subjects too.*

Q **I've now realised that I take a rather analytical view in terms of managing my team (I'm a lawyer by the way) and concentrate heavily on getting what you call the hygiene factors right. One of my team works very independently of me. She simply gets on with things and only involves me when it's absolutely necessary. I now have a feeling that I should be acknowledging that and thanking her. Is that the right thing to do? Or might she see that as interference?**

A *I'm sure that she won't see your appreciation as interference. We all like to feel valued and involved, so it's highly likely that she'll actually be delighted. In fact, letting her know that you really value her contribution and thanking her for her hard work will probably inspire her to keep it up.*

13

Do they ask for it?

If we assume people are workshy, untrustworthy and lack commitment and then proceed to treat them as though this is how they are, they'll probably start to exhibit this kind of behaviour.

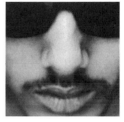

The following idea derives from some interesting business research. It can easily be adopted in our personal lives as well as our working lives.

YOU CAN TRUST ME

Let's look at the business angle first. The motivation guru Douglas McGregor produced one of the most enduring pieces of management theory: Theory X and Theory Y Management. This has become part of management business vocabulary. According to McGregor, managers tend to make assumptions about the people who work for them. These assumptions fall into two broad categories.

Theory X managers have little faith in their employees. They believe that people dislike work and that money and fear are their only motivations. They also believe that employees can't be trusted and that they lack creativity except in finding ways

How could you be sending Theory X messages to your team or family? Talk to them about it and ask them to tell you whenever they get that feeling. How can you positively change how you deal with someone to demonstrate that you believe them to be Theory Y? Think hard about how you're communicating. Are you concentrating on getting your own ideas across and criticising other people's, or are you encouraging and supporting the ideas of others?

round management rules. Theory X is, of course, a self-fulfilling prophecy. If you make assumptions about people and treat them as though that is how they are, then that is how they're likely to behave.

Theory Y managers believe pretty much the opposite. They believe that people need to work for psychological as well as economic reasons and that they're motivated by recognition and achievement, easy to trust, seek responsibility and so creative that they represent the best source of ideas in the business. This, too, is a self-fulfilling prophecy.

McGregor believes that people tend to be a mixture of the two theories, with Theory Y behaviour predominating unless external pressures, such as failing to meet targets, move them towards Theory X.

Interestingly, if you were to ask any employee which of the two profiles most closely describes them, the vast majority will choose Theory Y regardless of what grade or level in the organisation the person is.

BUT WATCH OUT FOR THEM

However, if managers are asked whether or not they agree that there are more Theory X attitudes and behaviours displayed by employees at operational levels than they would ideally like to see, the answer is nearly always 'Yes'. However, since all employees describe themselves as more Theory Y than Theory X, then if we accept the self-fulfilling prophecy principle it stands to reason that Theory X behaviour only arises as a result of the way managers treat their staff.

IDEA 26, *Am I hearing you?*, is about influencing people by listening. It might give you some further insights into Theory Y behaviour.

Try another idea...

On the face of it this seems nonsense, since these managers have no doubt described themselves as predominantly Y. I have a theory about this. Suppose that every day at work the managers are unintentionally sending Theory X messages to their employees because of the way in which they communicate. If managers don't listen to their employees, tend to tell them what to do all the time and suppress their ideas because of their own seniority and increased experience, then they're probably sending a message that they don't trust each individual and their team to perform.

This can now be transposed into our personal lives. We trust our children, but do we really display this trust? For example, if we check every Thursday that our son has remembered his football boots, then will he bother to remember them? If we trust him to remember, he may be more likely to remember or take responsibility for the outcome if he forgets (which might serve as a reminder for next time too). More seriously, if we display an attitude that says, 'You don't want to do school work because it's too much effort', then children might adopt that attitude. If, on the other hand, we treat children as though they understand the need to learn and want to get on with it, then hopefully they'll develop Theory Y attitudes and behaviours.

'People become motivated when you guide them to the source of their own power and when you make heroes out of employees who personify what you want to see in the organisation.'
ANITA RODDICK

Defining idea...

57

Q **I've realised that I wasn't giving the most junior member of my team at work any responsibility whatsoever. She was simply required to carry out orders. I thought of something extra she could do and gave it to her as an objective without telling her how to do it. I've been told that she's floundering and worried about coming to me for help. That's not what's supposed to happen is it?**

A *Remember that she's probably used to Theory X treatment, so she may need more support. Sit down with her next time and ask for her thoughts on how to achieve the objective and then listen to her figure it out. Try to remember not to interrupt with advice. Then leave her to get on with it.*

Q **I've always reminded my daughter to pack her recorder on music day. I decided to trust her and I even managed not to look and check that she had it. She's forgotten it twice so far. Do I continue to trust her in this respect?**

A *You may want to think a little more widely. Are there other areas where your behaviour demonstrates a lack of trust? My advice is to keep going and to try some other positive and encouraging behaviours and I'm sure she'll soon get the hang of it. Be sure to notice when she does remember her recorder and give her praise and encouragement!*

14

What comes first?

We have many needs in life, and some won't even surface until others are truly satisfied. To help others fulfil all their needs is a key role for a great leader.

I only became aware of my need to make a difference when I was earning enough money to survive, paying the mortgage, living in a reasonable home, in a loving relationship with friends and family, and generally feeling happy.

BEING SHIPWRECKED

Imagine that you've been shipwrecked. You regain consciousness laying half in and half out of the water, spitting out seaweed and the odd fish. As you look around you realise that you're on an island and the only survivor. Assuming that there's no means of escape, the first thing that you're going to want is food and water – without food you have days to live, without water just hours. Having found food and water, you may decide that you want to find a shelter to protect you from the elements and any wild animals that lurk around. You may also want to learn how to make fire and be able to catch the odd fish. Having done all this you might begin to

Here's an idea for you... **Think of someone with behaviour that you'd like to see change and establish why they behave like that. What payback do they get? When I was much younger, I used to smoke. Why? Because my friends smoked, I thought it was cool and I wanted to be part of the gang. I was also shy and asking people for a light was an easy way to start a conversation. My parents used health reasons to try and make me stop, with zero chance of success. One of my daughters smoked up until recently and I also wanted her to stop for health reasons! I had to work at keeping my mouth shut almost daily.**

feel lonely and think about exploring the island to find some companions. You're lucky! You find a complete village and, instead of eating you, the natives welcome you. You probably then wonder what role you can play in this village and may become the English teacher, highly regarded by all. Only then might you begin to think about your real passion in life – painting. Your ship was travelling to Hawaii where you were going to paint for six months before returning home to sell your paintings. It was what you'd always wanted to do – it was your dream. Nevertheless, what was the likelihood that the first thing you would look for on regaining consciousness was your paints and easel? No chance, because survival and basic comforts need to happen first.

We often try to fulfil what we think are someone's needs, when in reality we don't have a clue what they actually need. We all do things for a reason that works for us. I certainly don't know too many people who do things to deliberately fail! Imagine that at work you have someone reporting to you who's the best sales person in the company, who loves what he does, earns good money and manages to take Friday afternoons off to play golf with his friends. You think he'd make a good manager and decide to promote him, and sell him this golden opportunity based on how much more money he'll make,

It's easy to do things just because you feel you should. See IDEA 11, *Who's pulling your strings?*

Try another idea...

how he'll have more authority and how he won't have to travel so much, etc. You think you've given him a great chance. Now think about this. The skills required to be a great manager are very different to those of a great sales person – he may fail. He's used to being the best, but this position will be lost. What happens about his golf with his friends? And isn't selling his passion? The outcome of this promotion could be that he's no good as a manager, doesn't make the grade and ends up being fired. Now he may have to change his entire lifestyle because he doesn't earn as much money. What's actually happened here is that you had no idea what his needs were and made a decision without understanding those needs. If you want someone to change their behaviour, you'll find it virtually impossible unless you first understand why they're doing what they're currently doing.

'**What is necessary to change a person is to change his awareness of himself.**'
ABRAHAM MASLOW, psychologist

Defining idea...

How did it go?

Q I often wondered why my attempts to stop my husband smoking weren't working. Is it ever too late to change a habit such as that?

A *I don't think it's ever too late, but if he's been smoking most of his life then it's probably more of an addiction than a habit, which may be more difficult. However, there are things that you could do if, and this is a big if, he wants to stop. First help him to establish why he smokes and then see what can be done to replace those needs. For example, one of my problems was shyness. How else could I approach people without asking for a light? How else could I become 'cool' and part of the gang? Develop other tactics because if there's nothing to replace them it's easy to slip back.*

Q You said that a leader's key role is to help people fulfil their needs. Could you explain that further?

A *Once all your basic needs are fulfilled you can really start to think about what your real passion is, your purpose if you like. Mine is to take all my life experiences and use them to help each person I meet. I want to make a positive difference to their lives. If I worked in a big organisation then I'd like my boss to encourage me to find ways that I could do this. This would encourage me to become more of whom I'm capable of being, and help me to deliver even more because I'd be delivering 'with passion'. Whatever we're truly passionate about is likely to be where we can become outstanding. And in my mind, helping each person become the best they can be is what leadership is all about.*

62

15

Whose idea is it anyway?

Great teamwork is encouraging other people's ideas and then building on them. We immediately have a supporter – the person whose idea it was! We may also end up with an even better idea.

Do we acknowledge good ideas? Or do we tend to jump on them and say why they won't work, or barely listen before leaping in with what we've decided is a far better idea?

ADDING OR SUBTRACTING?

We have unbelievably active minds, and most of us want to share our ideas. After all, those ideas may solve a problem, present a new opportunity or get us out of trouble. However, how often do we feel that nobody's listening to our ideas and that everyone else gets more airtime than us? How many of our great ideas that we so kindly share are either hijacked or totally lost. I occasionally sit in and watch business meetings and I'm saddened by the lost opportunities that I see. I watch someone suggest a way forward and wait with bated breath for someone to acknowledge that idea. Not to necessarily agree but to say, 'Hey, that's an

Here's an idea for you... **Next time someone comes up with an idea, listen carefully and see if you can find a way to build on it. Before you build on it remember to tell them that you think their idea is interesting. This is critical and if you miss this bit out it may sound as though you're actually coming up with a different and better idea. Forgetting to support their idea can create the kind of problems that we looked at earlier. Remember: support then build.**

interesting idea, we could look at that.' Nothing! So what happens? You see this person switch off and mentally say, 'Well you're not interested in my idea so why should I show interest in yours?' They either withdraw or when someone else comes up with an idea they do their best to shoot it down. The crazy thing is that many of the people in that room actually think that it is a good idea *but they don't say anything.* It's as though they expect the person to be a mind-reader and know that their idea is valued.

This sort of communication is the quickest way I know to suppress creativity and innovation. I see it happen again and again, and then the boss complains that nobody comes up with any ideas. I feel like shouting, 'Why don't you just listen, support and encourage the ones that you hear'.

ADDING IS BETTER

A far more productive way to deal with an idea that's been expressed is to be encouraging by acknowledging its value and then, if possible, build on it. For example, suppose a colleague comes up with the idea of launching a new product that's really easy and cost effective to produce. I might then say, 'I think this sounds like a really interesting idea and what might make its launch even better is if we could combine it with the launch of this other product, which we have been looking at but are unsure whether it has a market; together they could really take off.' The first person might then say, 'That's a great thought and if we launch in July at the start of the children's holidays it could take off pretty quickly.' What happened was that I took the original idea and extended it. What you now have is synergy and teamwork. You have two people working together and extending ideas so that, hopefully, the ideas are thought through more thoroughly and are more effective as a result.

When someone does come up with an idea, be sure that you properly understand what it is that they're suggesting. Remember that words mean different things to different people. See IDEA 28, *Have I got that right?*

Try another idea...

Sadly, this is rarely what I see. The people who come up with ideas are usually ignored, the person who speaks the loudest gets her ideas through, or the person with the most power and authority wins. And this is true in families too. Often the youngest or most 'junior' person's ideas aren't seriously considered. A pity, because they can often come up with the germ of a good idea that – if listened to, supported and built upon – could become a great idea and the young person will feel encouraged to be even more creative the next time.

'Ideas are like rabbits. You get a couple and learn how to handle them, and pretty soon you have a dozen.'
JOHN STEINBECK

Defining idea...

How did it go?

Q **How do you deal with a child who only comes up with absolutely ridiculous ideas?**

A *The first thing that I would want to know is why this is the case. Is it being done deliberately because your child feels that you haven't listened in the past? Try asking, 'If you knew that we're going to go along with whatever idea you suggest, what idea might you now put forward?' The other thing that could help is that no matter what idea your child comes up with, don't put it down or tell your child that it's silly. See if there's any part of that idea that you could actually work with. I think that your child will only have to realise a couple of times that you're taking them seriously before the creative juices start flowing.*

Q **There's someone at work who always puts down other people's ideas. It's not that she comes up with her own; she simply tells everyone that their idea is no good and won't work. How should we deal with her?**

A *Give her some feedback – constructively of course! From what you're saying I don't know if she's simply unaware of the impact she's having on others or if it's deliberate. I really wouldn't do anything other than sit down with this person one-to-one and explain the impact she's having on the individuals concerned. Also explain that what she's doing is actually suppressing ideas. Few people consciously want to be destructive and it's often just an unfortunate pattern that they've developed.*

16

Please, let me think!

Think things through properly and you'll make better decisions. Moreover, helping others to think things through will improve their decisions and at the same time enhance your leadership and relationship skills.

Each of our decisions, however great or small, are preceded by thought, be it phoning a girlfriend, letting the dogs out, choosing to go to university and study philosophy, or emigrating.

QUALITY THINKING PRODUCES QUALITY DECISIONS

Many of us live and work in environments that aren't conducive to real thinking. And it stands to reason that if the quality of our thinking is poor, then the decisions we make and the actions we take are also likely to be poor. The results of our actions will therefore also be less than optimal.

So perhaps it would be helpful if we could create an environment for ourselves, our colleagues and our friends that is suitable for thought – let's call this a 'thinking environment'. I first came across this idea when I read an inspirational book by Nancy Kline.

Here's an idea for you...

Take an issue that's really important to your children and invite them to think it through by sharing their thoughts with you. Promise that you're not going to give them advice but merely act as a catalyst to help their thinking and the decision that follows to be as good as it can be. (If you've never done anything like this before they may feel a bit suspicious and probably won't believe you at first, so don't let them down by doing anything other than listening.) Your interest will help them and they'll be entirely responsible for the decision they take.

At some point we all will have methodically thought a decision through and worked out what we should logically do. However, sometimes logic says 'Do A' when our gut-reaction is 'No, that's not right.' This is our intuition telling us to do something different, but because we can't analyse it we go down path 'A' then quickly realise that the better decision would have been 'B'. So, when I talk about thinking I don't just mean analytical thinking, I also mean intuitive thinking.

Now, although most of us can manage to set aside some time and progress in our thinking on our own, there's no doubt that, like so many things, a bit of help from our friends is invaluable. This is because, as well as silent thought, we also need to articulate our ideas to make sure that our thinking is sharp and defined as opposed to 'woolly'. So, the first component of a thinking environment is the knowledge that we're being listened to. We need to know that we have someone's undivided attention. In other words, that someone is completely focused on what we're saying, with their eyes on us continuously and their whole demeanour saying, 'I'm fascinated by what you're saying and listening hard while you come to your decision.'

Your full attention is vital when you're helping someone to think because if you start to do something else like tidying and say, 'No, do carry on I'm still listening', the other person's thought process is interrupted. They'll then become convinced that what they're saying isn't interesting and that you're bored – the likelihood is that their mind will just close down.

Another way to help someone reach their potential is to show them that they're valued. See IDEA 4, *The impact of appreciation.*

Try another idea...

So, to help someone think a decision or course of action through, find a quiet room, sit them down comfortably and give them your undivided attention for as long as it takes for them to get to where they want to be. Then, when you have an important decision to make, ask them to do the same for you. Remember, the decision and subsequent actions are only as good as the thinking that precedes them.

'When people talk, listen completely. Most people never listen.'
ERNEST HEMINGWAY

Defining idea...

Q **I tried this with my twenty-year-old son who is, in my opinion, about to make a bad mistake about where he's going to live. I assured him that I wouldn't give advice and that I just wanted to help make sure that he'd thought the decision through. It was very difficult, but I kept my faith and listened while he went over his thoughts. It was good, but he missed out big areas that he should be considering. I've got to tell him about them, haven't I?**

A *You've done so well so far and it may be that now you've opened up his mind to a different way of thinking he'll become aware of some of these considerations himself. In a week's time you might like to ask him how valuable he found your listening to him. If he found it valuable you could ask his permission to share with him some information that you thought he may have overlooked. After you've given him this information you could ask him if he'd like to think it through again at some point.*

Q **My partner has a problem at work and I encouraged him to think it through. He got very emotional and I found that difficult to deal with. What should I have done?**

A *Ideal! Just kept listening. The mind needs to be able to release emotions so that it can think straight. If you continue to listen to your partner he'll begin to move through his pain and gradually be able to think clearly again. Learn to be comfortable with someone being upset. They'll surely be able to move through it. However, only listen, don't start directing – you're not a qualified counsellor!*

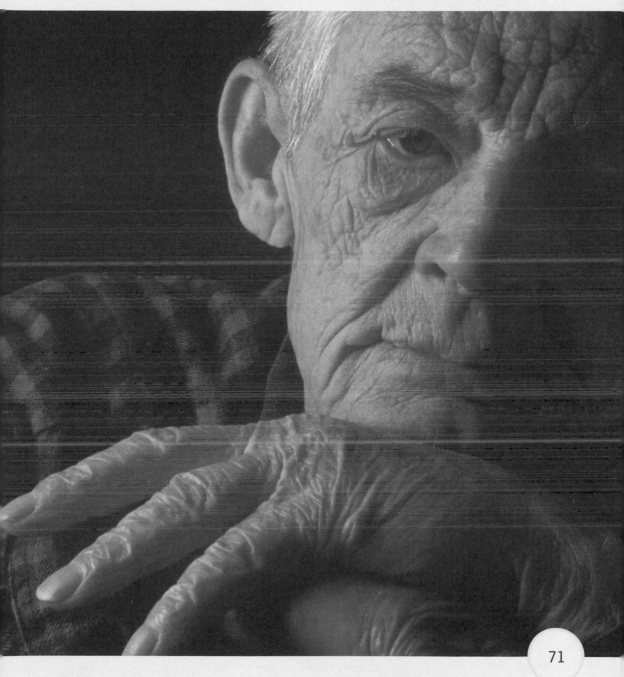

17

Encourage to inspire

The motivation to change has to come from within us. People can, of course, encourage us in a number of ways, but ultimately motivation isn't an external energy.

If we accept that we can't control what's outside of us, then it stands to reason that we can't make someone else do anything.

THE POWER OF ENCOURAGEMENT

Where does motivation come from — externally or internally? I believe that motivation comes from within and that therefore we can only motivate ourselves. However, I've always found that if we have certain things in place and we behave in a way that's encouraging, supportive and appreciative, then it's possible to create circumstances in which people are far more likely to feel motivated to act in particular ways.

Think about how we behave with very young children. Imagine you're in a room with some friends and there's a toddler there who takes her first steps whilst everybody's watching. What do you think would happen? No doubt everyone will be clapping, cheering and cuddling the toddler. It stands to reason that the child

Think about the systems of recognition you have in place at home or at work. Take an aspect of your children's behaviour that you want to encourage, and make a conscious effort to notice and praise that behaviour. Don't do this simply by buying tangible presents, but take the time to really show them how you feel. This also applies at work – don't leave it to formal systems to recognise achievements, make sure that you take the time to thank people for their efforts and to appreciate their commitment.

will then want to do more of this. Moreover, when she does she'll get the same reaction, and so on. It's only when children get a little older, possibly around school age, that our focus tends to shift to highlighting behaviour that we don't want to see, instead of recognising, appreciating and supporting the behaviours we do want to see. For example, we expect children to behave well and so we hardly notice when they do, but boy do we notice when they behave in a disruptive manner. Often children find that they get far more attention for less acceptable behaviour so, guess what, they do more of it!

TELL THEM IN THE WORKPLACE AS WELL

We all like a sense of achievement. I don't know anyone who doesn't like to say, 'Yes, I did that', whether in respect of a piece of embroidery, getting a hole in one or an achievement at work. How long does it take word to get round at work that someone's made a mistake? Probably not long at all. Members of a team that's not working well together will publicise errors as they seek to disassociate themselves from them. Fixing the problem also involves the rapid transmission of opinions and suggestions. Compare this with how long it takes people to receive recognition for their successes.

There's often no system in place to make sure that people's achievements are publicised. Yet one of the greatest motivators for people is simple recognition that what they're doing is valuable to the organisation and that they as individuals really count. An individual's achievements can be recognised with a simple thank you; repeating that expression of gratitude in front of colleagues is highly motivating and has the following secondary benefit.

IDEA 12, *What made you do that?*, looks at another aspect of motivation at work.

Try another idea...

Generally, people welcome responsibility. They prefer to achieve objectives rather than simply carry out tasks. They want to develop and take on even greater responsibilities, and are far more likely to want this if they feel that their achievements will be recognised and valued.

'No person can be a great leader unless he takes genuine joy in the successes of those under him.'
REVD. W. A. NANCE

Defining idea...

How did it go?

Q   **I feel ashamed that I've focused so much on the negative aspects of my children's behaviour. But how can I change my approach and still avoid the bad behaviour?**

A   *If we're not getting enough attention for the things we do well, then we'll start to do more of the things that we do get attention for, even if they're 'naughty' and result in a scolding, which is better than nothing. So, if you greatly increase the appreciation levels for behaviour you want to encourage, and decrease the amount you pick up on the things you don't want, you'll begin to see a shift. It takes time, but stick with it and you may be pleasantly surprised.*

Q   **The members of my team work remotely so I'm not in constant touch with them and can't see how they're working day to day. I only really see the final results of their work and these are either right or wrong. I obviously have to point out when their reports are incorrect and this can cause some real upsets. But how can I keep them motivated by giving them praise without being insincere when I don't know what they are doing?**

A   *If they rarely hear from you, aside from when you're pointing out where they've gone wrong, then it's not surprising that they can get upset, as they've probably worked really hard to get the report done. You can show them that you value them by picking up the phone and speaking with them regularly, asking how things are going, asking them how you can help and thanking them for their constant dedication even though they're remote. If you do this they may begin to share any confusion or concerns they have at an earlier stage, leading to an increase in correct reporting.*

18

Liberate your thinking

Many people believe that there are barriers limiting their ability to succeed or achieve their maximum potential. These barriers need to be removed in order to allow a different and clearer way of thinking.

Limiting assumptions hinder our success. They are beliefs that we have about ourselves, others and our situation that limit our thinking and so inhibit our performance.

FREE YOUR MIND TO THINK

As a result of my mother leaving when I was a few months old and being sent away to boarding school at the age of seven, I carried around the belief that I had no value, that I wasn't good enough. If someone had helped me to remove that barrier, I could have expanded my horizons and thought in a hundred different ways. One powerful way to help someone overcome limiting assumptions is to ask an incisive question. For me a really useful question would have been, 'If you knew that you are good enough, what would you do right now?' Many possibilities would have sprung to mind. If I knew that I am good enough I could pursue a career that I

Here's an idea for you... **Think of an issue that's troubling you and figure out what's preventing you from resolving it. Now form the incisive question that will remove the barrier and allow you to think freely. To do this first take the words 'If you knew that...' and then turn the barrier into a positive and place it in the present tense. For example, 'If you knew that you can create the perfect relationship with your partner, how would you behave differently?' Ask the same type of question of someone you're trying to help at home or at work.**

know I would be good at – public speaking. If I really knew that I am good enough I could start on the process of achieving my vision of owning my own company and owning the property I wanted for my children and myself to live in...and so on. Note that it isn't necessary to change my belief, but that this question allows me to think differently by jumping the invisible barrier in my mind.

This use of an incisive question can be an incredibly powerful tool in helping yourself or others to tackle new challenges and remove the problems that they believe are holding them back.

Here's a business example where a single incisive question opened a floodgate of possibilities to a chief executive who was my client. He asked me to dinner so that he could decide if he wanted me to become his personal coach. His major preoccupation in his division of a very large company was their difficulty in hiring and keeping the best people. That was to him the key problem in turning round the performance of the division. I asked him the question, 'Tell me, if you knew that you could turn this organisation into a preferred employer, one that's not just successful, but with a reputation such that people are desperate to come and work for you, what would you do differently from what you're doing now?' There was a ten-second pause and then he said, 'Penny, I really don't know.' I smiled and encouraged him to think further, 'I do really understand that but if you did know, how would you go about it?'

IDEA 49, *Involve them all*, might also help someone who's limiting their thinking, and to understand more about how the brain works look at IDEA 44, *How do I persuade them?*

Try another idea...

AND WORK OUT WHAT TO DO

The chief executive said that if he knew what to do, he'd start by sharing his vision with each of the division's 300 people, individually and in groups. After continuing for about twenty minutes he stopped suddenly and said, 'Where the hell did all that come from?' What had happened was that this man had been thinking about what needed to be done for so long that he assumed he didn't know the way forward, and pathways had formed in his brain so there seemed no way he could get fresh thoughts. All I'd done was remove that assumption by asking what he'd do if he did know the way forward. So, incisive questions are an excellent way to remove barriers or limiting assumptions so that we can think more freely.

'There are indisputable beauties in this world. The human mind is certainly one. An Incisive Question to free it is another.'
NANCY KLINE, personal development trainer

Defining idea...

How did it go?

Q **I believed that what was holding me back was the fact that I had to stay in the job I hate so that my family and I could continue to live in the manner we had become accustomed to. So I asked myself, 'If I knew that I have everything I need to find a job that I love and maintain our standard of living, what would I do?' And you're right, the ideas started flowing. But I can't expect my family to take the same attitude can I?**

A *Perhaps you need to sit down with them all and explain how you feel and what you're considering. Their concerns may well be a series of limiting assumptions. Try using incisive questions to help them clear these barriers so that they can think more freely about new possibilities.*

Q **Can I use this idea with my son who isn't doing very well at school and has started to think he's stupid?**

A *Definitely. See if you can get him to think about what he'd do if he knew that he is clever. So the incisive question might be, 'If you actually knew that you are extremely clever, how might you approach your work differently?*

19

Boost your thinking power

It's exciting and liberating to think beyond our self-imposed limits. Above all, it gives us the opportunity to make a real difference in our own lives and the lives of others.

The most powerful improvement in our capacity to think creatively for ourselves comes not from the encouragement or advice of our friends, but from their carefully chosen questions.

SILENCE IS GOLDEN

In order for us to think at our very best, it helps to have someone listening to us. I've found that even when I've invested a huge amount of time in thinking about a particular idea or issue, as soon as I start to share it with someone who gives me their time and undivided attention it begins to grow and expand in a much more exciting way.

A number of the ideas in this book are based around listening and so it'll come as no surprise that I consider this to be the principal element of communication and

Here's an idea for you... **Find someone you know who's been trying to make a decision about something for ages, but keeps getting stuck and giving up. Ask if they'd like to sit down and think it through again, but this time with you acting as a coach and asking them a few questions to help them think. Also explain that you won't be giving them any advice. Then choose a comfortable place where you won't be disturbed and just see what happens.**

helping others to reach their potential. But if we take the time to combine it with focused questions, then it becomes truly exciting. We can then start to create a path forward to help to uncover some of the beliefs that might be preventing them from moving towards their goals and dreams.

LESS IS MORE

The questions that will really help someone to open up are very simple. Sometimes people say to me that it seems too easy and they want to add a bit more. However, keeping it simple is key here because the focus isn't on what *you* want to achieve. The power is with the thinker and it's up to them to go wherever their mind wants to take them.

First, simply ask them what they'd like to think about. Then listen. Listening is extremely powerful so never feel that you're doing nothing. Often this question will be enough to create all kinds of breakthroughs. Nevertheless, when they start to dry up, ask if there's anything else that they think or feel about the subject and keep asking until you're sure there's nothing else. Then ask what they'd like to achieve from this thinking session.

Once it's very clear in their words what they want, use their words to complete this sentence, 'What might you be assuming that is stopping you from achieving…?' Then listen. If they dry up, ask them the same question until they really have no more to say. You'll probably end up with a list of assumptions, which could be anything from 'I'm not good enough' to 'I might get the sack' or 'I might not pass the exams'. Then ask them which of the assumptions they think is the most important one to them. There's a big lesson here, which I've learned many times over: we're only interested in their most important assumption and it may well not be the one you thought!

Now that they've discovered the block that's obstructing their thinking, you have a key to help them open the door. This key is the incisive question. This may all sound out of the ordinary, but it can be one of the most powerful thinking tools if you stick to the ground rules: only ask these particular questions and listen with your entire being without influencing the other person's thought process.

To learn more about assumptions see IDEA 18, *Liberate your thinking.*

Try another idea…

In IDEA 9, *We are what we decide to be*, you'll find some more advice on how to formulate incisive questions.

…and another idea…

'*Advice is what we ask for when we already know the answer but wish we didn't.*'
ERICA JONG

Defining idea…

83

How did
it go?

Q **I decided to give this a try with a friend who has wanted to change her job for ages. We've talked about it many times and she's always asking for my opinion. In the past I've told her what I think but she hasn't done anything about it. So I suggested that I try this idea with her. We only got as far as me asking her what she felt she might be assuming was stopping her from finding a job she really wanted when she suddenly had all sorts of ideas and is now enthusiastically following her plan. Where did I go wrong?**

A *What makes you think you went wrong? Remember, this process isn't about you. The power is with the person who is doing the thinking and if they make a breakthrough or want to stop at any point in the proceedings, then that's exactly right. It sounds to me like you did an excellent job. Well done.*

Q **One of my team came to see me at work because they weren't sure what to do next to get a difficult project back on line. Normally I'd have given them advice based on my experience, but I decided to use these principles instead. I was shocked to realise that anxiety about the consequences of getting it wrong has stopped them from trying new ideas in the past. It was an excellent lesson for me, and they came up with a great idea. How could I have been so blind to this before?**

A *They were blind to it as well as you. Their assumption will have been limiting their thinking process and therefore their ideas won't have been of the highest quality. This will in turn have knocked their confidence still further. It's amazing what happens when we begin to really listen.*

20

Don't live your life by accident

We do have a choice about how we live our lives. For example, we can choose to focus on work. Alternatively, we can place a higher priority on family and leisure. Whatever our choice, how do we get the balance just right?

Here's a way of establishing whether you have the balance you want or whether you need to make some changes.

CHECK THE CURRENT SITUATION

There are 168 hours in a week, and you probably spend around 56 of them in bed. So, this leaves 112 hours for living in. Draw a table comprising three columns and three rows, resulting in nine square boxes. In each box write down an activity or area of your life where you currently spend your time, such as Friends, Relationships, Family, Alone Time, Work, Spirituality, Vision, Personal Growth, Health, Hobbies, Leisure, Creativity. If you need more squares just add them. Also include areas that you wish to get involved in, such as Fitness or Travel.

Here's an idea for you...

Create an action plan. All too often we talk about wanting to get fitter, visit friends or take up a new hobby, but another year passes and we never seem to get around to it. Head up columns with the areas you wish to work on, then create two rows for listing exactly how you intend to go about the change and when you intend to achieve this by. Also include a 'completed' box. The key is to break the path to success down into small, realistic and achievable steps.

Now add the number of hours in a typical week that you spend in each of these areas. Then convert these numbers into a percentage of 112 and write the percentages into the appropriate boxes.

That's your starting point. You may wish to ask your partner or a work colleague to take a look at what you've written to make sure that you're not indulging in any wishful thinking. If the percentages are just as you'd like them to be, then well done – there's no need for you to continue with the rest of this idea.

One person I did this exercise with decided that he was spending too many hours watching television and too many hours working. The area that suffered as a result was his box marked Wife and Family. Following this realisation he resolved to refrain from watching TV between Monday and Thursday. He also committed to telling his boss that he was only going to work late three evenings a week and that he was leaving each Wednesday and Friday at five o'clock. He decided to ask for support from his team at work and to sit down with them to look at their work–life balance and to ask them what he could do to help them get their ideal balance. He planned to take his wife out for dinner once a month and decided he would tell his two sons that every other weekend they could have half a day of his time to do anything they wanted to do, provided it didn't cost more than a couple of DVDs. His commitment to action made this exercise really work for him and his family.

Ensure that your work–life balance isn't affected by your disbelief in what you can achieve. Try IDEA 15, *Whose idea is it anyway?*

Try another idea...

PLAN THE FUTURE SITUATION

Now look at your own table and decide on the areas where you want to make adjustments. Remember that you'll need to counterbalance each area where you wish to raise the percentage. And resolve to get started on any activities that you've added that you currently don't do. Now translate the percentages into hours and see whether you think you have a feasible plan.

'We're so engaged in doing things to achieve purposes of outer value that we forget that the inner value, the rapture that is associated with being alive, is what it's all about.'
JOSEPH CAMPBELL, US expert on mythology and comparative religion

Defining idea...

How did it go?

Q **I'd really like to spend more time with my daughter, who lives half an hour away. Lunchtimes would be best for her because she works most evenings and weekends, but how can I ever manage it as I work during the day?**

A *You could start by explaining the situation to your manager to see if there's the possibility of some flexible working to allow you an extended lunch break or perhaps an afternoon off once or twice a month? Also, perhaps your daughter could come over to you sometimes?*

Q **I really want to get fitter so that I'll be able to play with my grandchildren and really have some fun with them. I've tried joining a gym, but it just doesn't seem to work. I start with good intentions, but then find it difficult to find the time to go. What would you suggest?**

A *It's often easier to make time for the things we enjoy most. Perhaps your difficulty in finding the time has more to do with the appeal, or lack of it, of the gym. Have you considered other ways to improve your fitness that might fit more easily with your lifestyle? For example, replacing a regular car journey with walking or cycling, taking the stairs rather than the lift, exercising whilst at home in front of the TV? I've just started playing golf and I love it – I feel really good about the exercise.*

21

It's your choice

We live the lives we choose to live. We react to people the way we choose to react to people. However, what we believe about ourselves can limit our choices and make us feel like victims of circumstance or mistreatment.

My mother ran off when I was a few months old, and I was eighteen when I next saw her. I was packed off to boarding school at the age of seven.

My father worked exceptionally hard. This meant that, with the exception of Sports Day in summer, he and my stepmother rarely managed to visit me at school. Sadly they missed many things that were important to me – plays I was in, sports teams I played in, swimming displays I captained. My friends' parents managed to visit them far more often. What beliefs did I create about me as a consequence? I believed I had no value and that I wasn't good enough, since even my own mother seemed to think she was better off without me.

I left school at eighteen, fell in love, got engaged at nineteen and married at twenty to someone sixteen years older than me. The marriage didn't get off to a great start when my husband invited his ex-mistress to join us on the honeymoon! Despite

Here's an idea for you... **Do you know who you are? Are you so busy being what your employer, children or partner want you to be that you've lost sight of who you are and what you want from life? Ask yourself this really simple question and write down the answers that first spring to mind. What do I really want from life? Then ask yourself this. If you knew that it is OK for you to do what you want in your life, how might you go about it? This will help you to identify things that you can do whilst acknowledging all the other aspects of your life that you need to consider.**

this, I had three lovely children in quick succession. I ended up having three nervous breakdowns in the space of two years and went through a period where I lost my memory and tried to kill myself. I also managed to hand over about a third of the large sum of money my father had settled on me on my marriage. I wasn't in good shape when I came out of that relationship.

Still, I met someone else pretty quickly, got married again and had three more children. That marriage was happy for a while, but ended when my husband had an affair with my best friend while I was pregnant! I came out of that marriage having handed over half of my remaining money to my husband. The lawyers took a good chunk as well.

I then spent six years on my own bringing up my six children and doing many different jobs just to pay the bills. In spite of this, this was one of the happiest times in my life.

Then, you've guessed it, I met someone else. I thought that I'd definitely got it right this time so I married again. I was wrong again. In many ways, this was probably the unhappiest marriage of all. It went badly wrong after about three years. On top of this, my second son died at the age of twenty-six. That divorce cost me my remaining money.

So, there I was on my own with no money just debts. I'd lost all my confidence and was a mess.

HOW DOES A VICTIM BECOME A VICTIM?

It's easy to identify the repeating patterns in this story. I developed certain beliefs about life and me as a result of my parents' background and the way I was brought up, such as men are in charge of everything, including money; men make the big decisions and women go along with them; women run the house, keep it clean, look after their men and are great mothers to their children. Combine these with my underlying belief that I wasn't good enough and you have a predictable outcome. I spent all my time trying to please my husbands and never achieving this, never being good enough. And I blamed them for not treating me well.

I ended up feeling very unhappy, very 'hard done by' and a complete victim of circumstances. How could I be so unlucky? Why did I always choose powerful, charismatic men who ended up walking all over me? Then, through reading, attending workshops and exploring new possibilities, it eventually dawned on me that as I was the only common denominator in this story it had to be something to do with me. This was very hard to come to terms with, but think about it for a moment. If I believed that I wasn't good enough, then how would I behave in any relationship? As if I wasn't good enough. I had to take responsibility and acknowledge that I'd educated my husbands to treat me that way, yet also complained when they did! On realising this, the most exciting thing for me was that I had everything I needed to change my life. Change didn't depend on other people. All I had to do to change my life was change my way of thinking.

There's more on knowing who you are in IDEA 6, Creating our own reality.

Try another idea...

'Nobody can make you feel inferior without your permission.'
ELEANOR ROOSEVELT

Defining idea...

How did it go?

Q **A big problem in my life is my son's attitude towards me, his mother. Like your ex-husbands, he expects me to be his housekeeper and feels he doesn't need to contribute. Are you saying that it's my choice that I wash and iron for him, etc.?**

A *Yes, that's exactly what I'm saying. You can choose to stop doing it. It's as simple as that.*

Q **This one hit a nerve with me because I've always had an expectation that my boss always knows best. I now realise that I have to change how my current boss treats me and be more assertive in the relationship. Is there anything else I should consider?**

A *Good on you, but don't forget that you can't change how your boss behaves. You can only change yourself. Your boss will then have choices to make.*

22

Who is in charge of your life?

It's too easy to live your life the way others want you to live it. Even scarier, you may not even recognise that you're doing it.

It took someone saying, 'Could the real Penny Ferguson stand up please?', for me to realise that I didn't know who I was and that I didn't actually own my life.

WHO AM I?

I guess it started when I was a small child, when I did what my parents told me to do. Because my parents were older and therefore wiser I automatically assumed that they knew best. Even when I was rebellious, which was exceedingly often, I didn't truly feel that I was my own person. I was just rebelling because I resented the rules that were being imposed, not because I was choosing who I really wanted to be. I spent most of my life trying to be what I thought others wanted me to be. I was always trying to fulfil their expectations.

Here's an idea for you... **Pick one day next week to be your day to do whatever you want. Decide not just what you're going to do, but also how you're going to feel and look. Set aside thinking time to ask yourself, 'If I knew that I own my life 100%, what might I be or do differently right now?' You could do this while taking a walk, lazing in a bubble bath or playing golf. Don't write your answers down yet – just open your mind to new possibilities.**

When I was married to my first husband, I spent time trying to be all that I thought a wife should be. On top of the standard things like washing, ironing and cooking, I used to run his bath, put out his clothes each day, drive him to and from the station to save him from having to park, and so on. The more I did, the more he expected of me. But as soon as I had three children aged under three, I didn't have the time to continue doing all these things. He complained and I felt a failure. To compound this, I was noticeably failing in trying to be all that a mother should be.

After I left my second husband and was bringing up six children on my own, I became a fee earner, an employee and an employer. It was towards the end of my third marriage that it hit me that I didn't know who I was.

THE STARTING POINT

I couldn't believe how hard it was to define 'Me'. I'd completely lost sight of who I was. In fact, I'm not sure I ever knew who I wanted to be. This was when I sat down and did some exercises – including writing my own obituary! – so that I could recognise who I wanted to become. And I tried to visualise my future life, in order to identify what I wanted to do. So I was now clear on the who and the what, even if the how wasn't clear. I then took ownership of those decisions and for the first time in my life felt that I had the chance to choose to live my life the way I wanted to. I knew that having identified for the first time who I was and what I wanted to do, the how would become clear. Looking back, I realised how many things I'd done to please other people and consequently I'd missed lots

Think about how you wish to be in your special relationship. Try IDEA 31, *What will become of us?*

Try another idea...

of glorious opportunities. This filled me with remorse. I'm fully aware that this is a pointless emotion, but it was still one that I had to work hard to let go of.

I now own my life totally and whatever the circumstances I recognise that this is actually where I'm choosing to be, how I'm choosing to feel and how I'm choosing to react. If it's off track then I'm choosing it to be that way. If I'm in an abusive relationship, that's my choice. If I'm behaving in a way that denies my values, then that, too, is my choice.

'*Most powerful is he who has himself in his own power.*'
SENECA

Defining idea...

How did it go?

Q **When I'm not being a wife and mother I'm acting as an unpaid chauffeur, counsellor and finance manager. How can I find a whole day for me when I can't even find an hour?**

A *First ask yourself whether this is absolutely how and who you want to be and accept that you're currently choosing your life to be this way. If you say that you can't find a day, then that's your choice. And if you feel empowered by that choice, great. If you don't, then you don't own your life. Sit down with your family and tell them how you feel and that you want one day for you.*

Q **When I read this chapter I burst into tears. I realised that I really don't know who I am, especially at work. I'm only in this job because it's where my parents pushed me to be and now I think I've left it too late to change jobs as I'm not qualified to do anything else. Can I *really* still change?**

A *That's an interesting couple of assumptions – that you've left it too late and that you're not qualified. I only started to change my life at fifty, with no money, no qualifications and no confidence! What do you most enjoy doing? When are you at your happiest? When do you feel most alive? Look at these areas first and, most importantly, recognise that where you are now is exactly where you're meant to be. You'll have learned some valuable lessons on the way, so how can you use them? Do the exercises recommended earlier and keep asking yourself, 'If I knew that I absolutely can do this, what might I do differently today?'*

23

Talk in their terms

We spend a lot of time communicating with people in the hope that we'll be able to influence them in some way. We know the outcome we're seeking and the action we'd like them to take. Here's a way to maximise your ability to influence people.

If we listen carefully to people and understand their point of view, we'll be able to present our ideas in their terms and the outcome is more likely to be successful for everyone.

LEARN FROM SUCCESSFUL SALESPEOPLE

When it comes to selling, I've often heard that you need the 'gift of the gab'. In my opinion, successful salespeople are far better at listening than talking and that's where they put their emphasis. They really listen to a client in order to learn about the client's business, areas of concern and future aims and where the client believes he needs help. Then the salesperson is able to offer their services in a way that the client can identify with. Moreover, the salesperson is able to use the client's

Think of an idea that you're trying to get your boss or partner to accept. When you sit down together, first ask for their thoughts about the situation. How do they feel about it? What outcome would they like to see? What would be the most important elements to them in achieving the outcome? Really listen to what they have to say then convey your understanding of what they've said as words can mean different things to different people. How often have you been in deep conversation with someone then halfway through said, 'Oh, I didn't realise that's what you meant.' Next ask them if you could share your thoughts with them. Concentrate on presenting your idea using their language and aligning it as closely as possible with the outcome that they'd like to see.

language. This demonstrates that they're interested in the client, that the client's real needs are of importance to them and that they're prepared to invest time in supporting the client. If we want to build long-term relationships with people, then I believe that this is what is important.

Of course, it also means that the salesperson is able to stress the benefits of their product or service in a way that really means something to the client, and the discussion is therefore much more likely to result in a sale and the development of a long-term business relationship.

Can you imagine building any kind of trusting relationship with some of the salespeople who phone you or knock on your door and insist on talking for at least ten minutes without taking a breath before giving you an opportunity to speak?

On the other hand, think about how you feel when someone has really listened to you and then responded to what you've actually said instead of simply telling you what they'd like to see happen. When we feel that someone is sufficiently interested in us to listen, then we tend to react far more receptively.

It's always a good idea to check your understanding of what someone's said to be sure that you're both coming from the same place. Check out IDEA 28, *Have I got that right?*

Try another idea...

LISTEN AND INFLUENCE

The same applies when you're talking a situation through with your partner, children, colleagues or friends. If you'd like to share an idea with them, first ask them for their ideas, establish why their ideas are important to them and really listen to what they have to say. You can then ask to share your idea with them as they're more likely to listen if you've already listened to them. In addition, you're now aware of what's actually important to them, so you can present your idea in their terms, stressing the relevant points.

'A good listener is not only popular everywhere, but after a while he knows something.'
WILSON MIZNER, US screenwriter

Defining idea...

Q **I have a great idea to suggest to my sister, but she's very strong-minded and doesn't really respond to other people's ideas. I don't want to force anything on her, but I'd really like her to listen and evaluate what I have to say. I know that if I ask her to listen to me, she'll say that she doesn't need advice. What can I do?**

A *Remember that listening is the key to getting your ideas heard. So firstly ask her how she feels about this area of her life and what she'd ideally like to see happen and why. Then ask her if you can share your thoughts. When you do, be sure to use her language and stress the benefits that will be particularly relevant to her. Remember, when you truly understand where she's coming from you may end up thinking that she's right!*

Q **I tried your idea with my boss. I wanted to tell him about an idea of mine so I asked him his thoughts first and then told him mine. I even tried to stress the benefits that I'd thought of beforehand. But he wasn't interested. Where did I go wrong?**

A *Firstly, although this idea is here to help you successfully put forward your point of view, it isn't a guarantee that your idea will be embraced. However, it may be worth thinking more about his thoughts on the matter. If you thought about the benefits beforehand, did you really listen to him and put them into his language? Sometimes, if we 'practise' we automatically say what we planned, as opposed to really responding to what we've heard.*

24

Why plan your life?

I spent most of my life believing that I was doing what I wanted with my life. Then I realised that I wasn't my own person at all as I'd never actually sat down and thought hard about how I really wanted my life to be.

Do you really have a vision for how you want your life to be or do things just happen? Do you ever feel as though life is passing you by? And are there times when you say 'If only...'?

HOW MUCH DO YOU VALUE YOU?

I spent a large part of my life focusing on what I didn't want – getting myself into situations and knowing that I didn't want to be there. If anyone asked me what I did want, by the second sentence I was telling them what I *didn't* want! If anyone suggested creating a vision for my life I thought, 'What a waste of time and how would that help?'

Here's an idea for you... **Set aside an hour and find a pen, some paper and a quiet place. Now imagine the best six months of your life. Not six months that you've already lived or the next six months, but six months of your dreams. Picture yourself at the age of ninety-five telling your great-grandchildren about this incredible six months that you're living, what you're achieving, how happy you are, what a fantastic job you're in, what wonderful relationships you're enjoying, what a beautiful house you're living in, and so on. Describe all this in as much detail as possible. Now put this somewhere that you can see it every day, read it each morning and see what happens. Even better, each day ask yourself, 'If I knew that there is one thing that I can do today that will move me closer to my vision what might that be?' Then do it!**

By the age of fifty, having had six wonderful children and having had three less than wonderful marriages and having lost all the money that my father had left me, I found myself with debts and no confidence. I was an emotional wreck and I suspected that this wasn't entirely what I'd envisaged when I was younger! When a good friend and colleague suggested I do a vision, I never thought that it could change my life. If I'm completely honest, I did it to humour her! After I'd completed the task, I laughed at what I'd written because it seemed a complete impossibility and was so far from where I was at that point in my life. In the ten years since, I've rewritten my vision three times because I have exceeded it each time. How I wish I'd met that friend years earlier.

Think of it this way. Have you ever bought a new car thinking it's not a car that everyone else has, yet the day you collect it and start driving it's as though everyone else has had the same feeling. Suddenly there's twice as many of the same car on the road. The reality is that they were always there; you just didn't notice them before. The same thing happens when you create your vision for your life. Suddenly opportunities begin to appear as if by magic. But they were always there, you just didn't see them before.

STEALING YOUR DREAMS

It's so easy to have your dreams stolen, and sadly the people who steal them the most, after you of course, are the people closest to you. At the age of eighteen my younger daughter's dream was to become a jockey, and when she went to live with her father he persuaded her that this wasn't a viable future. He loved her so much that he wanted the best for her and he thought that being a jockey would be a tough life where she would earn no money and have to be in the top of her profession to get anywhere. He also thought that it wouldn't be good for her back, which was weak owing to an accident she'd had when she was younger. After becoming an extremely successful sales manager, she came to work with me and began to rethink her dream. She worked shorter hours to qualify as an amateur jockey, came second in the first race she ever ran and then went on to win the second! Unfortunately she'd left it too late to ever qualify as a full jockey. Effectively, loving her as we did, we stole her dream. When I told my best friends what I wanted to do, they all tried to stop me – they thought it was too risky and that I could lose everything. Are you allowing the people closest to you to steal your dreams or could you be stealing theirs? Think it. Dream it. Do it.

Think about the balance in your life – too much work and not enough time for you? Try IDEA 51, *Living in the moment*, or IDEA 20, *Don't live your life by accident*.

Try another idea...

'The great thing in this world is not so much where we are, but in what direction we are moving.'
OLIVER WENDELL HOLMES

Defining idea...

105

How did it go?

Q **I found this really difficult, as I'm so used to thinking about what my family wants. I was amazed that I had to keep saying to myself, 'What do you really want?' Isn't this selfish?**

A   *I don't think so at all. The things that we're passionate about are normally things that we're really good at. Do you want your children to do the things that they're really good at and care deeply about? I feel sure you do, so why not do the same for you.*

Q **What do you do if your partner has a totally different dream to you?**

A   *I'd suggest that you each do this exercise individually and then share your dreams with each other. After all, diversity is a wonderful thing. You can then plan how you can support each other in fulfilling these dreams. It's really important that you don't share your vision until your partner's completed theirs. If they really love you, they're less likely to tell you what they want if it appears to conflict with your dream.*

25

When feelings hamper thinking

How many times when you've been furious or deeply upset have you said or done something that you bitterly regret? I bet you still squirm when you think about these moments.

Too often, I look back at my life and remember something that I've said to one of my children and really wish I'd never said it.

STICKS AND STONES

'Sticks and stones can break your bones but words can never hurt you.'

This little piece of wisdom was thrown at me a lot when I was growing up, and I fundamentally disagree with it. Bones can heal, but words can stay in your heart and mind forever. The saddest thing for me is that the people we hurt the most are the people closest to us. Why? Because we're emotionally involved with them, and because they seem to know which buttons to push to have us bouncing off the ceiling. Consequently we react, and probably in the least useful way because we're angry or upset and therefore not thinking clearly. We're thinking in extremes –

Here's an idea for you...

Next time someone's angry or upset, stop what you're doing and give them your undivided attention. Find somewhere where you won't be interrupted and just listen – no agreeing, disagreeing or advising. Fix your eyes on them all the time, encouraging them by the way you're looking at them. The only question that you can ask is, 'Is there any more that you think or feel about ...?' And once they've calmed down and got everything off their chest, you can ask what they'd like to do next and then do whatever's appropriate.

black/white, yes/no, good/bad – and we're highly likely to react in a very emotional way. This will probably make the situation a lot worse.

I remember the impact that the change in a client's behaviour had. She was a lovely woman, but very fiery and reactive and constantly at loggerheads with her boss. This meant that she often got passed over for great projects, which was having a serious downward spiral effect – no new project, furious row, worse relationship, poor quality thinking. This in turn would lead to the next project being handed to someone else, more fury, a worsening relationship, and so on. Her performance was suffering because her thinking was being constantly interrupted by negative emotions. During the programme, another situation blew up. She, her colleagues and her boss all went for a drink after work and her boss started to have a go at her about these work issues in front of her colleagues. (Entirely inappropriate management behaviour, but we'll leave that for now!) Her colleagues went quiet, expecting her typical reaction, which was to completely explode and say things she'd regret. Instead, she took a deep breath and once he'd finished she said quietly, 'Tell me, is there any more that you think or feel about this?' Everyone erupted into laughter, but most importantly she'd done two things: she'd allowed her boss the opportunity to expel his anger so that he could free his mind to think clearly, and she'd also done that for herself.

EXPRESS, EXPRESS – AND THEN THINK

When someone is furious or deeply upset they won't be able to think clearly. They have to be allowed to move through it before they do anything else. So, what you need to do is just

Remind yourself that if you care about allowing people to think well, giving not getting is what's important. See IDEA 1, *Who you are is what you get.*

Try another idea...

listen. Anyone in sales will know that the first rule regarding handling complaints is always 'absorb the pain'. This isn't to say that when we're angry or upset we always make bad decisions, but it's highly probable as we're likely to be reacting emotionally. If someone is having a go at you it might not be easy to simply listen, but think back to an occasion when you tried to defend your position. How helpful was that? Probably not very, and the emotions almost certainly hung around a lot longer than they needed to. Moreover, hurtful things may have been said, which will have exacerbated the situation. The knack isn't defending; it's listening and encouraging someone to get everything off their chest. And once they truly feel heard they'll be able to start thinking clearly again. Even if they say something that's grossly unfair from where you're sitting, remember that at this moment it's very fair as they see it. If something is genuinely unfair, but you allow them to express it anyway, once they've calmed down they're likely to admit this themselves.

'*Speak when you are angry – and you will make the best speech you'll ever regret!*' LAURENCE J. PETER, Canadian educator and writer

Defining idea...

How did it go?

Q   **What if the person they're upset with is me? Are you seriously suggesting that I keep listening, even if what they're saying is totally unfair?**

A   *Yes. My third husband used to have a real go at me, take things out of context and twist my words. I'd invariably end up in tears, nearly incandescent with rage. But I never won! The minute I lost control he was in the driving seat and I'd end up wondering if I was going barmy. Stay focused on the outcome that you want - a pleasant evening, to be happy together, whatever. Then keep listening until all the upset is spent. You then have a chance of sorting it out, especially if you can persuade your partner to listen to you in the same way.*

Q   **When I'm upset or angry I burst into tears, and as I work in an environment dominated by men this really doesn't help. How can I deal with this?**

A   *The easiest way to deal with this sort of issue is to label the problem. If you become upset in a meeting and think you might cry, say so. I mean it! Tell them that you care passionately about what you're about to say and that you may get upset. When you do this you take the pressure off you and the thing that you fear subsides. If I'm about to give a talk to a large audience I may tell them that I'm nervous as then I don't have to fear it and the nerves seem to disappear.*

26

Am I hearing you?

When helping others to come up with ideas and make their own decisions, it works best if the language being used is theirs, not yours. It's extraordinary the influence you can have just by listening to people and even by simply getting them to repeat what they've said.

When we hear ideas in our own words they're more likely to resonate and influence us. We're more likely to want to pursue them.

LISTEN ON THEIR TERMS

Have you ever found yourself in a situation where a friend suddenly comes up with an idea to improve their life in some way and you're left thinking, 'But I told them that, months ago?' I certainly have, and I've felt frustrated when this has happened – I could have helped them much more if I'd influenced them at that time. However, the fact of the matter is that most of us come up with ideas at about the time that we're ready to move forward. So, if someone else is telling us what to do, we probably won't embrace their suggestions or feel committed to achieving them because they don't resonate for us. I believed for a long time that a nephew of mine should go to university, and I told him so. It was two years before he asked me about getting application forms!

Here's an idea for you...

Think of someone who's been coming to you for advice on, say, their life, relationship or job so that they will be happier, and try asking them an incisive question such as, 'If you knew that you can create a solution that will move you forward towards a happier and more fulfilled life/relationship/job, what would you do differently?' Then just listen. If they dry up, encourage them to continue by asking them what else they would do.

However, if we encourage others to explore their thinking, talk through everything they're hoping to achieve and come up with ideas and options for moving forward, there's a good chance that they'll want to get started with their plans as soon as possible. A really helpful way to move towards an outcome that will solve a problem, create a new initiative, provide a way forward, etc., is to resist the temptation to share your ideas and instead help them to explore their own mind by asking them searching and incisive questions. You can then offer support and encouragement using their language, so that they feel comfortable with where they're going.

NO TRANSLATION NECESSARY

The effect of hearing our own voice and words expressing ideas is incredible. We feel much more comfortable with what we hear than if it were said by someone else. Thinking quietly on our own can be helpful, but actually verbalising our thoughts seems to clarify them further and is much more likely to create positive action.

Have you ever thought about what you wanted to say to someone in advance and then opened your mouth and been frustrated or embarrassed by the fact that what you say doesn't really capture what you were thinking

IDEA 18, *Liberate your thinking,* **suggests incisive questions that might help people work out an action plan.**

Try another idea...

or what you meant? I certainly have, and sometimes the consequences have been really upsetting. It may have been because your thinking process wasn't complete, as this only begins to happen as you hear yourself express your thinking out loud. So how much better would it be to hear all our thoughts clearly before we approach the situation.

By offering ourselves as a listening partner, we perform a valuable role in helping a friend, colleague, partner or child clarify their thoughts. They will then be able to focus clarly and commit to action.

'The most called upon pre-requisite of a friend is an accessible ear.'
MAYA ANGELOU

Defining idea...

How did
it go?

Q   **A friend of mine has been unhappy in his relationship for ages and constantly asks me what I think. He's never taken any of my advice, so this time I decided to ask him an incisive question. He just said that he didn't know what to do and that was why he was asking me! Why didn't it work?**

A   *Sometimes when people have been blocked in their thinking for ages and have become used to receiving advice, their mind is out of practice in terms of pushing its thinking boundaries and needs some extra encouragement to get kick-started again. A question that often works is, 'But if you did know, what would you do?' Otherwise, just listen to him and let him talk about how he feels. If you're patient, he may well start to come up with ideas that will work for him.*

Q   **My little boy came to me the other day and said, 'Mummy, I can't build my Lego train.' I remembered your words and said to him, 'If you knew that you could build it, what would you do first?' He immediately said that he would separate the bricks into different shapes, so I suggested he go and do that first. He ended up building most of the train himself, with only a little help from me. Is this the sort of thing that happens all the time when you try this approach?**

A   *Well, it certainly happens often. I've had this kind of feedback on my programmes from many parents who are amazed at just how much more ability their children have than they realised, perhaps because they haven't given that ability enough of a chance to shine through. Well done. Keep it up and I hope you continue to be amazed.*

27

Tell me how I'm doing

If we truly want to become the best we can be – in any field of endeavour – then we need someone who can tell us, openly and honestly, how we're doing.

To become a better boss, colleague, parent or friend we need to ask the people we manage, our colleagues, our children and our friends about our progress.

WHAT WE DON'T WANT TO HEAR!

Being a leader, in its broadest context, is about recognising that the minute you influence another person you are, in fact, leading. If you wish to become an outstanding leader you need to know how you're doing – you need frequent feedback. However, we have parts of us that we're not yet aware of – limiting beliefs and hidden talents. We have areas where we know exactly what our strengths and weaknesses are, but we do our best to hide the weaknesses because we want to pretend that we're better than we are. And we have areas where we're blind or just have an inaccurate picture of how we are. For example, someone may think that they're a really caring and open person who people find easy to talk to, yet one day

Here's an idea for you... **Ask your children how they see you as a parent. Also ask how they'd like you to change, and ask your team at work the same. When a client of mine did this, he was shocked to discover that several things that he was doing, which he viewed as useful, were actually upsetting his team. He also thought that if he did this exercise he'd lose credibility, yet his team's motivation improved almost exponentially. Remember, if people won't tell you anything then you're either perfect or they're scared of you!**

somebody tells them that they're really very scary and people only tell them what they think they want to hear.

So, it's not always easy to receive really open and honest feedback from others, especially if it's not what we want to hear or conflicts with our perception of who we are. And the even scarier bit is that at work it's the people who actually report to us and are more junior who can give us the best and most accurate information. And if you want to know how good a parent you are, your children are the best people to tell you how you're doing. Have you ever asked them what sort of parent you are and what they'd like you to do differently so that they feel more enabled to become even better family members or individuals? I asked my children this after I started on this path of learning, expecting them to ask for things like more pocket money, more freedom or fewer rules about coming home on time. They really surprised me because they asked for things like more time for them to really talk to me, to be able to share their problems without me promptly telling them what I would do, allowing them to be themselves and trust them more, and much more besides. It wasn't easy but I'm sure it helped me to become a better mother. I began to understand that, without even knowing it, I had been becoming my mother and that my children were experiencing all the frustrations that I'd experienced in my childhood. I wasn't setting a great example as a leader.

CRITICAL INFORMATION

In many ways the skill and openness to ask people to tell you how you're doing is probably the most important thing you can develop. It's certainly the most courageous, and you'll undoubtedly hear things that you don't like, don't want to hear and will violently disagree with. You're likely to want to defend yourself, explain why you did things the way you did and generally behave like a cat on hot bricks. But don't! To tell a boss that he's not managing you as effectively as he could for whatever reason is not likely to be easy the first time. Corporate suicide isn't a popular pastime, and telling the boss where he's getting it wrong could be just that. In my experience, however, most people want to be the best they can be. They want to be great leaders. The problem is that we don't ask the people who count how we can improve. If each and every one of us took 100% responsibility for being the best we can be, then asking how we're doing would become a way of life. Change the way you communicate and be open to all that you hear. Allow people to say what they need to tell you without getting defensive for, whether you like it or not, their perception is their reality.

Think about how you treat your colleagues, friends or family. Do you trust them to be honest with you? Do you value their opinions? Try IDEA 13, *Do they ask for it?*

Try another idea...

'We judge ourselves by what we think we are capable of. Others judge us by what we have already done.'
HENRY WADSWORTH LONGFELLOW

Defining idea...

How did it go?

Q **I've been thinking about this, but haven't had the courage to do anything yet. I thought I'd start with my children before my staff. What would you recommend?**

A *It doesn't matter – just start! Facing your children, however, may not be easy. My eldest daughter once gave me some devastating feedback. She said that she didn't like me always buying her things or that when we went out I always paid. She was beginning to resent me because I wouldn't let her contribute. At this point in her life she was broke. I thought I was helping and making her life easier. We had a very emotional discussion and I asked her how she'd like things to change. We now have a very different relationship and I thank God that she was brave enough to tell me how she was feeling and I was receptive enough to hear it.*

Q **If I ask my team to give me feedback about the way I manage, won't it look as though I'm a weak manager?**

A *In my experience the exact opposite is true. Everybody likes to be needed and if your team think that you need their help to become the best you can be, then they're more likely to see that as a strength. Also, if you acknowledge that you're not always perfect and that you're happy to learn from your mistakes, they'll be much more open about their weaknesses. Hopefully your work environment will become one of openness and trust, where mistakes become a learning opportunity rather than something to hide and shift the blame for.*

28

Do I have that right?

Good communication enhances relationships. The mood of a family dinner or the success of a business meeting can be transformed when we actually understand each other rather than simply think that we do.

Have you ever been involved in a heated debate with someone when it suddenly dawns on you what they actually mean and you realise you agree with them after all?

TESTING UNDERSTANDING

Sometimes, even though we're listening to what's being said, we're not actually hearing what is meant. Let me give you an example. Have you ever been somewhere such as a conference or parents' evening where the keynote speaker or the head teacher are on stage and addressing the audience? You're listening but you're beginning to think you must be missing something because you're not entirely clear about what they're talking about. You wonder whether there's a paper that you should have read or a letter at home that has gone astray. However, everyone else seems to know what's going on and so you don't want to make a fool of yourself by asking a question.

Here's an idea for you... **Next time you're not entirely sure that you've grasped the idea that's just been explained, ask a question. Try, 'Can I just make sure that I've understood correctly and that what you're suggesting is...?' Alternatively try, 'When you say that, do you mean that you want me to...?' Better to test your understanding than to waste your valuable time.**

If you're lucky, some brave soul will raise their hand and say something like, 'When you said that you're now planning on moving forward with the project, did you mean.... ' The speaker is then likely to either say, 'Yes, that's exactly what I mean' or 'No, what I meant was....' At this point you can feel the relief in the room as everyone begins to understand what the speaker meant, and you realise it wasn't just you that was feeling lost. But what if nobody had asked a question to clarify the situation?

The English language is full of words that are difficult to define. We know their basic meaning, but they can take on a different emphasis dependent upon the context or the aim of the speaker. For example, if your child asks you to pick them up from school early the next day you may wish to ask what they mean by early, otherwise you could arrive an hour before your usual time when in fact your child only meant five minutes early.

CONFUSION REIGNS

Imagine that you've just had your appraisal at work and your boss has highlighted a couple of areas in which you need to 'do better'. You

For more about ensuring that we've really understood what someone means see IDEA 47, *Egg timer peace.*

Try another idea...

think this means that you need to do things like write a more detailed report and maybe attend more departmental meetings. At your next meeting with him, however, he tells you he's disappointed. And when you ask why, he says that he was expecting a more committed response from you. If only you'd realised that what he really wanted was for you to send in weekly updates to keep him informed, to communicate with other departments on a daily basis and to include some additional recommendations in your report. If only you'd asked what he actually meant by 'better'!

So why didn't you? For some reason we're often reluctant to ask in case it makes us look silly. But how silly do we look when we go away and put heaps of effort into doing the wrong thing? So, asking questions to test our understanding, to ensure that we're very clear about what someone is explaining to us or asking us to do, is a very useful habit to develop.

'Much learning does not teach understanding.'
HERACLITUS OF EPHESUS

Defining idea...

Q **Can you overdo this? When someone asks questions in our monthly meeting I can almost see the boss getting angry as if to say, 'Surely I've made that clear, this is just a waste of time.'**

A *I personally don't believe you can overdo it. Unless you have a full and clear understanding about something then you're likely to make poor quality decisions. How about 'labelling' the question before you ask it. For example, 'What you said there is really useful, but knowing how important it is that we get absolutely the best outcome for the company/team could I just test my understanding of...?'*

Q **I have twin boys who are young teenagers and, despite looking identical, very different from one another, one being quiet and gentle and the other being much pushier and assertive. They're always arguing, and listening to them it sounds as though they're from different planets. Is there anything I can do to help? I normally end up getting cross and telling them to go and argue outside where I don't have to listen to it!**

A *How about letting them know how you feel when you hear them arguing? Then suggest they do an exercise. Ask them each to write down all of their brother's strengths. They must be as positive as they can and aren't allowed to say anything negative. Now ask them what they might be able to achieve in life if they put those strengths together. Ask the question, 'If you knew that you could talk to each other in a way that means you can begin to truly understand what the other person is saying, how might you communicate differently?'*

29

But I asked you to listen to me

When someone's thinking hard in order to reach the best decision about something, we can fall into a trap called 'giving advice'. This often hampers the thinker and can be devastating.

Instead, the person helping should remember that listening is their critical role. They don't need to express their views or ask any questions except, 'Is there anything else you think or feel about this?'

BREAKING THE THINKING RULES

I encourage people to form thinking partnerships, where one person listens to another thinking something through. On one occasion, I was demonstrating how to do this by thinking through something with support from Kirsten, a colleague. The issue I was keen to work on was how to teach this way of thinking to young people.

Here's an idea for you... **When you're the listening partner in a thinking partnership, you might find that there's something potentially important that they may be missing. In my experience this is usually due to a lack of information. We know what happens if you volunteer advice at the time, so don't. What you could do, after you've told them how well they've been thinking, is say that there may be some insights that you could share with them in a week or so. By that time they may well have thought about these issues too.**

This is an area that I care about passionately and I believe it could make a real difference. I'd been thinking about it a lot, but unsurprisingly I was being held back by the belief that I wasn't good enough to do this.

Kirsten used a simple incisive question to free up my thinking, 'If you knew that you are good enough, what would you do first?' My thinking took off and I replied, 'If I knew that I am good enough I would talk to some teachers to find out if they would be interested in the project. I would also talk to some parents, invite some teachers on to one of my programmes, and much, much more.' I came up with some wonderful ideas and I felt really energised and excited by the possibilities.

Kirsten was great and obeyed the rules by listening and refraining from giving out any advice. Afterwards I opened the conversation to the floor to ask them if they had any questions on the listening partnership process. There were a few, and then something happened that proved a huge learning point for the group and for me. Somebody said, 'Can we just broaden this out a bit, because I have a concern. Before you go and talk to teachers about this, have you taken this into account?' He then proceeded to delve right into the topic I'd been thinking about. What had he done?

As loud and clear as he could he'd reinforced my initial view that I wasn't good enough. He immediately told me where I was getting it wrong and then gave me advice.

The impact on me was huge. To everyone's amazement I burst into tears and for a long time afterwards I couldn't think about having anything to do with this project. In fact, I still haven't launched it! All that thinking time was completely undone.

The impact on him was equally significant. When he saw what he'd done and the group went on to discuss it, he realised that he was always doing the same with his teenage children. His children would think about something, decide what they were going to do and tell him about it. But instead of telling them that it was a really good idea and encouraging them, he would inevitably point out the things that they'd missed. He'd often wondered why this had such a negative impact on them, and this exercise dramatically demonstrated the reason.

You can influence people just by listening to them – see IDEA 26, Am I hearing you?

Try another idea...

'To listen closely and to reply well is the highest perfection we are able to attain in the art of conversation.'
FRANÇOIS DE LA ROCHEFOUCAULD

Defining idea...

127

How did it go?

Q   My daughter talks to me about some of her financial matters. I have no qualifications in this regard, but obviously I have some experience that she doesn't. I got her talking about the issue and asked the question, 'Is there anything else you want to say on this topic?' I was hoping that she'd reach her own conclusions. In the end she became frustrated and asked me straight out what she should do. What went wrong?

A   *Well done. You helped her to start her thinking. Sometimes you can ask another incisive question that will help to open up thinking still further. For example, 'If you knew that it is possible to obtain all the information you need to help you make the best decision for you, where would you start your search?'*

Q   My boss is just like this! I wanted his help in thinking through an issue with a customer. I'd hardly finished explaining the background when he told me what I should do and even started to make the first telephone call to implement his ideas. How do I handle this?

A   *Be open with your boss. Tell him what happened on that occasion. Next time explain that you want his help in forming your own decision. It might work. You could always demonstrate by offering to listen the next time he has a challenge to resolve. You might also explain to him that you would feel more motivated to take the action required if you were the one who designed the solution.*

30

Young people can think like giants too

When it comes to imagination, experience can be a handicap. As we grow older, our thinking can become increasingly restricted, preferring traditional thoughts to imaginative ones that could transform our lives.

It's amazing how we often think that unless someone has our knowledge and experience, their ideas couldn't possibly be as good as ours.

LET THOUGHT RUN FREE

Over the years I've learned many lessons based around this, and it's now my firm belief that absolutely everyone has the most incredible ability to think things through and produce wonderful ideas. Some people may not always be able to express them as eloquently as others, but their ideas are there if you look for them.

It seems to me that no group seems to be passed over for their opinions more than young people. Yet I'm sure that you'll have seen very young children display the most amazing imaginations – a saucepan and a stick can transform them into a knight, or an old petticoat and some high-heeled shoes several sizes too big can be

Try asking a young person in your life their opinion on something. Not on something that you might expect them to know a lot about, such as Spiderman or Harry Potter, but on something you imagine will be more challenging for them. If you ask their opinion and listen to what they say, you may well be surprised at what you actually don't know.

the key to becoming a princess. This imagination is eventually replaced by adult cynicism due to the passage of time, the burden of experience, the influence of conditioning, the focus of education, and so on.

I only wished I'd learned this earlier on in my life. However, I found that when I did begin to involve my children in developing new ideas, it had some wonderful results. They often came up with what initially seemed to be wacky ideas, but I didn't stop their flow by stepping in too early with practicalities. I would hear them out and then, having appreciated their contribution and praised their efforts, start to work with them to develop their ideas. We frequently ended up with a far more imaginative solution than I could ever have imagined.

DON'T DO THEIR THINKING FOR THEM

A client of mine had a problem with her son. He simply wouldn't go to bed at a sensible time. In fact, he wouldn't go to bed until it was time for his parents to retire for the night. His parents had no social life since they could never go out knowing that he would be asleep. After learning about the thinking partnership, my client decided that she was forcing her view on him instead of letting him work out the pros and cons of his behaviour. She sat him down, asked him to talk about bedtime and listened to his views. He more or less explained to himself why it was good for him to go to bed on his own and at the right time. When his bedtime came that night, he simply left the room and put himself to bed.

The impact of conditioning is looked at in more detail in IDEA 43, *How we view the world.*

Try another idea...

It's difficult not to assume that we know better than children and young people. In fact, listening to them is one of the greatest tests of our ability to listen as it's incredibly difficult not to give them advice. Remember that they won't think like giants until you treat them like giants.

'Every child is an artist. The problem is how to remain an artist once he grows up.'
PABLO PICASSO

Defining idea...

133

How did it go?

Q **This all sounds good in theory, but are you really saying that my ten-year-old child could provide ideas on financial investments or holiday destinations? I find that difficult to take on board!**

A *I admit that financial investments may be too challenging, but that's also the case for most adults, and it has more to do with a lack of information than a lack of imagination. You could broaden your questions to help the thinking process along – both your thinking and your child's. For example, if you want your child's input on a holiday destination, then why not ask them what facilities they feel would be useful for everyone or what type of accommodation they feel is most suitable, rather than just asking where in the world you should go. By the way, it may also be a good idea to encourage your child to think through the best use for their pocket money!*

Q **My children fight constantly and I find this very difficult. Once they were driving me to distraction, so I tried this idea and told them to sit down and think of how they could stop fighting. This just caused another argument, so where did I go wrong?**

A *There are two elements here. Firstly, it's not usually the best time to think about something when our emotions are running high. So, if they were still mad with each other they may have had difficulty focusing on ideas. Secondly, you could try a more positive focus and say something like, 'When you have different opinions about who should do or have something, if you knew that there are easier and quicker ways for you to sort things out, what other things might you do?'*

31

What will become of us?

In a relationship, life is apt to take over and we can begin to drift apart without realising that it's happening. Suddenly we can find that we don't actually know each other any more.

Setting aside time to develop a relationship, no matter how long we've been in it, is one of the most important things that we can do if we value this partnership as a lifelong commitment.

WHERE IS THE PROBLEM?

Let's look at a work situation first. There are two types of work activities: maintenance and development. Maintenance activities cover things that you do on a daily basis just to get your job done and include selling, taking orders, answering the phone, opening the mail, etc. Development activities are different in that they are one-off tasks and may include designing a new product, launching a new computer system, reorganising the office so that it operates more smoothly, and so

Here's an idea for you... **Sit down with your partner and agree that you want your relationship to be special. Then commit to the time that you're going to put into it, even if it means some rearranging of other activities. Ask each other what you really want from this relationship. How, ideally, do you want it to be? What needs to change for it to be that way? Don't just ask yourself what you really want. Ask the question, 'What do we really want?'**

on. Maintenance activities are things that we measure (*have we reached our sales target?*), are highly visible (*we haven't and everybody sees the figures*), affect the here and now (*how are we going to pay the salaries this month?*) and are low risk. Development activities, on the other hand, are the complete opposite. So, not surprisingly, everyone is drawn towards maintenance activities. Yet an organisation that doesn't invest time in development activities is liable to be overtaken quickly by its competitors and go bust.

A relationship is the same. When we first fall in love it's all about development activities – getting to know each other, exploring each others' hobbies, finding new hobbies that you could do together, and so much more. Then we move in together and perhaps get married. And what takes over? Maintenance activities like cleaning the house, working all hours to pay the mortgage, shopping and cooking. And then children come along and the problem escalates! The cost of living rises, we become full-time chauffeurs and household chores double. And what now happens to the time that we used to spend together developing our relationship and getting to know each other even better? That comes somewhere near the bottom of our priorities.

TAKE THE TIME

The things that always seem to suffer most are our relationships. How often do you find yourself writing in a Christmas card, 'We really must get together this year'? Worse, you then find yourself writing the same thing in next year's card. I have three activities that I do consistently at work. One is delivering workshops or fulfilling speaking engagements because if I don't do this I'm not earning enough money to pay the salaries today. One is selling and marketing because if I'm not doing that I may not be able to pay the salaries tomorrow. The other is developing my people. Which do I end up doing all the time? The first two, of course. Which is the most important? The last one, without question. So, now think about how important your special relationship is. Does it deserve the time to continually develop so that you can become closer and closer?

It would be worth doing your individual visions, encompassing every part of your life and not just your relationship. Try IDEA 24, *Achieving your vision*.

Try another idea...

'Stop acting as if life is a rehearsal. Live this day as if it were your last. The past is over and gone. The future is not guaranteed.'
WAYNE DYER, US motivation expert

Defining idea...

Q **I found this uncomfortable because my partner and I have begun to drift apart. Is it possible to really bring it back? I'm scared that we're now too different from the way we were.**

A *It entirely depends on whether you both want to bring it back. If you both do, then the answer is a resounding yes. Next create your visions, maybe independently, and then share them. Focus especially on the relationship bit and recognise that doing the full vision may give some insights into areas where you could develop new interests together. I lived with a boyfriend for three years and then due to various circumstances I left him. We've now started seeing each other again and both of us are looking at our relationship in a very different light – we're committed to development.*

Q **Surely relationships are more complicated than this. Sometimes you just make a wrong decision and it's time for you to move on. Are you saying that any relationship can be saved?**

A *No, that's not what I'm saying, and I agree that sometimes we can rush into things and get it wrong. Ask yourself whether the relationship is really over or whether it's just a case of the grass looking greener. It seems to me that we're inclined to give up all too easily – sadly I'm aware that there are occasions when I did, and I'd put my second marriage in that category.*

32

Your moment of choice

Your moment of choice lies in the gap between stimulus and response. Taking responsibility is the most empowering thing you can do once you truly understand its meaning.

It certainly worked for me. I changed my thinking and my life mainly by taking full responsibility for me. I stopped blaming others if things weren't as I wanted them to be.

RESPONSE-ABILITY – THE CHOICE IS YOURS

We often react to situations as if we only have one option. Once we recognise that we always have a choice we begin to feel in control of our actions and our lives in general. For example, what do you do if the phone rings? No doubt you answer it. But what else could you do? You could leave it to ring, let the answerphone click in, ask someone else to answer it, or even unplug it. These are all choices.

Now let's think about this in terms of our relationships. Let's just imagine that I'm at home one evening and I've decided to make a real effort and cook a fabulous

What happens when someone does something to upset you? Perhaps there's something that they keep doing that really gets you down, and you feel it's just not fair. Let me ask you a question, 'If you knew that you are able to choose an alternative response, how will you behave differently next time?' Make a decision and commit to it. You'll be delighted at how much better you will feel.

meal for my partner. The candles are lit, the music is playing, the wine is chilled and the food is almost ready. Then I hear the front door slam shut, a briefcase is thrown down, one of the dogs yelps as it's kicked out of the way and in he storms, ranting and raving about the dreadful day that he's had, his useless colleagues and how his boss has let him down. Then he says he doesn't want to eat and stomps off.

At that moment the phone rings and it's a good friend of mine asking if I'd like to join her down the wine bar for a drink. I reply, 'If you'd rung earlier I would have loved to, but my partner's just come home in a foul temper and put me in a really bad mood, so I wouldn't be very good company.' Now you might say that this is understandable, but did he put me in a bad mood or was that the response I chose?

Think about how else I could have responded. I could have listened to him, poured him a glass of wine and suggested he go and relax for a while. Alternatively I could have offered to run him a bath so that he could calm himself down. Or I could even have gone down to the wine bar.

WHAT OUTCOME WOULD YOU PREFER?

Had I chosen any of these other options, chances are that within half an hour we would have been sat down together enjoying my lovely meal. Instead, we're probably set for a full-on row and probably won't speak for days.

Now I'm not saying that we don't deal with issues. It's not about 'giving in' or 'being soft'. Although choosing an angry response at the time isn't particularly helpful, it's important that I talk to my partner and explain how I felt about his behaviour once everything is calm and perhaps a few days later. So, let's be clear, this doesn't mean hiding from challenges, but if we react as if someone else is pushing our buttons then we lose control of our life and let someone else run it.

In the gap between the stimulus and response is our moment of choice, whether it's deciding not to join our partner in a bad mood, choosing not to feel hurt when our children forget our birthday or choosing to go to a meeting with our boss even though we feel it's a waste of time. When we take responsibility for our behaviour and recognise that we've made a choice then we begin to feel in control, which is the most empowering feeling. It took me a long time to come to terms with the fact that I had choices in my relationships, that I didn't have to react to my husbands all the time and then blame them for the way I felt, but that I could make a conscious choice about my responses.

Look at IDEA 23, *Talk in their terms*, for help in explaining how you feel about someone's behaviour.

Try another idea...

'I am free because I know that I alone am morally responsible for everything I do.'
ROBERT A. HEINLEIN

Defining idea...

Q **Whenever I visit my ninety-year-old mother at the nursing home it only takes about ten minutes before I get angry. Nothing is ever right for her – the food, her haircut, the TV set, the fact that a grandchild hasn't visited for a week, and so on. How can I stay calm when she keeps moaning?**

A *It isn't easy, but think about what I said. What outcome do you want? If you get irritated then your mother will probably grumble all the more, plus you'll probably feel disgruntled for the rest of the day and may even take it out on another family member. I'm not excusing her behaviour, but why let it spoil your day? If you choose to remain calm then she may relax too and you may even start to enjoy your visits. Try starting a new pattern by mentioning some of the nice things about her or her surroundings.*

Q **I hate my job, but I can't leave because I'm in the family business and my dad says he can't do without me. I don't feel like I have a choice – I don't want to let him down, but I do feel trapped. What can I do?**

A *Although we always have a choice, that doesn't mean the choice is easy. First decide on your priorities. If you feel that you'd like to stay on and support your father, then you need to recognise that this is a choice and once you've made it choose how to approach the future. Will you choose a positive attitude and decide what will enable you to be the best you can be?*

33

Appreciating diversity

Appreciating a diversity of views and ideas can encourage us to let go of some of our limitations and enable us to think more deeply.

What is the first thing we do when we meet someone who thinks differently to us? We normally try to help them understand our point of view. Putting it more bluntly, we usually attempt to show them why our way is right!

CELEBRATE DIFFERENCE

Think about some of the most creative ideas you've ever had. They may have occurred to you on holiday in a new and exotic place, whilst walking somewhere wild and miles from anywhere, whilst skiing down a mountain or, like a good friend of mine, whilst out jogging. In other words, they often occur when your mind is removed from its day-to-day routine and given a chance to see things from a new perspective.

Here's an idea for you... **Next time you sit down with a group of friends or family to discuss something, find out what their feelings are about the matter rather than jumping straight in with what you think. Encourage everyone to listen to each person's thoughts until they fully understand why each person feels the way they do. Ask that nobody make any decisions at this point and suggest that instead they spend a few days with everyone's thoughts before coming back with any proposals.**

If we can accept this, then why aren't we prepared to let others take us to new and exciting places in our brains? What I'm talking about is giving ourselves the opportunity to share our ideas fully and be listened to without interruption, judgement or challenge. With a group of people, whether it's a family group or a business meeting, our best chance of creating a really innovative and exciting way forward is to have a mix of ages, experience, background and culture involved. And having accepted that this diversity will provide a wonderful opportunity for developing ideas, we then need to cherish the opportunity.

SEEK FIRST TO UNDERSTAND

Because of our tendency to gravitate towards people who are like us, we need to consciously open our minds to new thinking. In the words of Stephen Covey, an empowerment guru, we need to 'seek first to understand', which means we need to ask questions and encourage everyone in the group to share their views, without any feeling that they will be judged or ignored.

This is not just about hearing what they think. It's also about hearing why they think that way and what experiences led them to that place. When we understand why, we can start to build new perspectives in our own thinking, which is almost like being transported to a new viewing point.

I've observed many group discussions over the years and when people really start to work together as a team, exchanging thoughts and feelings without holding on tightly to their own ideas, the results can be amazing. It's a truly exciting process to watch.

Another important aspect of improving the way you think is covered in IDEA 34, *Thinking quality? Think equally.*

Try another idea…

Of course, one area where there can be a huge diversity in thinking is between parents and their children, particularly when the children are teenagers. I remember some of the struggles I had with my children when I really wanted them to understand my point of view because it came from experience and I wanted what was best for them. It didn't occur to me at the time to ask them more about what they thought and why. I simply felt I knew best. I really wish I'd known then, what I know now. These days, even when my children are thinking of doing something that I feel really concerned about, I listen and ask questions rather than try to force my point of view on them. The funny thing is, they're now just as keen to know what I really think and why!

'We should know that diversity makes for a rich tapestry and we must understand that all the threads of the tapestry are equal in value no matter what their colour.'
MAYA ANGELOU

Defining idea…

How did it go?

Q I tried this out by discussing a political issue with my son who holds an opposing view from mine. After a short time he became angry and it seemed better that we should agree to differ. What went wrong?

A *Are you sure you were really listening to him and trying to understand where he was coming from, rather than trying to change his view? Is it possible that he got angry because he felt that you were telling him that you thought he was wrong? Try again and be sure to simply listen without challenging him.*

Q My friend is married to someone who's totally different from her in every way, and they're constantly at each other's throats. It's become so uncomfortable that we no longer invite them for dinner because it's makes everyone else there uneasy when they just keep sniping. I love my friend to bits but I just don't know how to help her.

A *You haven't mentioned whether she's concerned by this and talks to you about it. If she does, your job is much easier. Why don't you get her to make her vision for the perfect relationship and then see what strengths she can find in what she has now – in relation to her vision. Help her to focus on her partner's strengths and ask, 'If you knew that you could take 100% responsibility for improving this relationship, what might you do immediately?' Help her to recognise and take ownership of her choice to be in this relationship and live it in this way. You also need to let her know why you no longer invite her for dinner – that's only fair, in my opinion.*

34

Thinking quality?
Think equally

We think best when we're with people we feel comfortable with. Feeling 'inferior to' or 'better than' someone limits this ability.

When people are thinking in a group, getting rid of issues of rank or hierarchy will improve the quality of the thinking.

It's also vital that the group leader, whether a parent or director, shows that they're completely open to listening to other ideas and not just determined to drive through their own. People can't think and contribute at their best if they feel that minds are already made up or that their view is unimportant.

WE'RE ALL POTENTIAL THINKING GIANTS

I was once helping a board of directors to produce their vision for taking their organisation forward. We'd all agreed that rank for the moment was unimportant and that everyone had an equal voice and, perhaps more importantly, an equal vote. The chief executive was plainly uncomfortable with the situation to begin with and

Here's an idea for you... **If you need to make a decision at a meeting then take care that you don't end up with too many ideas. You may lose sight of the best ideas or run with one that hasn't been properly discussed. Also, people get tired and the person with the loudest voice might get their idea through. If there are too many ideas, find a way to prioritise them and then discuss them one at a time. Concentrate on encouraging others to give their view on what's already been suggested, rather than just continuing to have everybody give their own opinions and ideas for actions.**

stayed somewhat aloof from the discussion. Also rather silent was the most junior member of the group who wasn't a director and was only there because his boss was ill.

Now there's always a danger that senior people will regard others who they deem to be of 'lower rank' as unable to talk at the required level and therefore won't invite them to contribute at all. However, true to the ground rule 'equal voice', the chair brought the junior person into the conversation. The result was explosive. She came up with an insight that staggered the rest of the board into silence. It was a thought that emerged more easily from someone who hadn't been engaged for so long on board matters. It was brilliant, and proved beyond doubt that you never know who's going to come up with the big idea in a discussion.

It really doesn't matter who we are, what school we went to or what friends we mixed with. Indeed, no aspect of our wealth or upbringing changes the fact that we're all thinking giants. We can choose to treat each other as such.

EQUAL VOTE IN THE FAMILY?

For more on keeping the outcome in mind see IDEA 46, *Yes, but what's the objective?*

Try another idea...

Nothing demotivates a teenager more than the realisation that they have no say in family matters. Is it unrealistic for them to be involved with important family decisions such as where the family lives or where it goes on holiday? I don't think so. A friendly thinking environment allows them to express themselves, and hopefully to listen as well as to contribute. If they're brought up to believe that their view is important, then they're more likely to make serious and useful contributions to discussions. We need to keep in mind the desired outcome of any family discussion or thinking session – a loving, mutually supportive unit. It can sometimes be incredibly powerful to accept the thinking of a junior member of the family, even though the parents may feel that an even better decision could be reached. True commitment and ownership of an idea can work even better than not having total commitment to a higher quality idea.

Ignoring the opinions of children or not inviting them to contribute doesn't allow them to help us to think. Moreover, judging that they can't help us to think can limit our own capabilities.

'There are people who, instead of listening to what is being said to them, are already listening to what they are going to say themselves.'
ALBERT GUINON, French dramatist

Defining idea...

How did it go?

Q This is all very well, but the eldest of our children, Peter, can talk nineteen to the dozen and it can be very difficult for anyone else to get a word in edgeways. This is particularly true of his youngest sister Lucy. How can we get a word in edgeways in a constructive way?

A *Try using a 'labelled shutout'. This means that you interrupt him, but explain the reason. For example, 'Thank you for that, Peter, but so that we can make a decision that is best for everyone, we need to give Lucy a chance to tell us her thoughts.' Then you can invite Lucy to speak. It might be good to ask him how good he feels about telling everyone his ideas. Then ask him if it might be nice to allow others the same opportunity.*

Q I don't get this. I'm the manager of my team and in the end I have the responsibility for its performance. I'm in my position because my judgement is deemed to be better than that of other members of my team. Why can't I continue to think things through myself and present my team with what we're going to do?

A *Managing your team to peak performance is more about developing them so that they can always think and act at their very best, whether you're there or not. Of course you have experience, but if you want to build a team that can continue successfully when you take leave or need to attend a conference for a few days, then encouraging their creative thinking is fundamental. Remember, 'The mark of outstanding leadership is not just how good a leader we are but how many leaders we develop.'*

35

We are what we decide to be

Three kinds of assumptions can hinder changes we wish to make in order to achieve the life we want and deserve: facts, possible facts and bedrock assumptions. We can think our way round all of them.

Thinking partnerships, where one person listens while another articulates their thoughts about an issue of concern, can help to push these limiting assumptions aside.

THREE LEVELS OF LIMITING ASSUMPTIONS

Limiting assumptions can be basic facts. For example, being a single parent. This may well be a fact but it doesn't need to limit how you think about and plan your life. Even 'facts' are fluid and 'removing them' at least temporarily from our thinking can generate unimaginable ideas and replace the feeling of being a victim with the feeling of having power to change. It's helpful to remember this whether you're thinking alone or as part of a thinking partnership. In the latter situation, the

Here's an idea for you...

Ask yourself what you're assuming is holding you back from all that you want to do with your life. It might be helpful to ask yourself the question out loud. Write down the first thoughts that enter your mind. Next create incisive questions that will remove these assumptions and then let your imagination soar. Make a note of all the possibilities for change in your life that you've identified and decide which ones to go for. This could be even more powerful if someone can listen to you and catch your ideas as they spring to mind. However, it's critical that they simply listen and don't try to give you any advice!

role of the listener is to help the thinker to remove the impact of the 'fact' on their thinking. Use an incisive question such as, 'If you knew that as a single mother you could find all the support you require, what would you do differently right now?'

Then there are assumptions that are 'possible facts'. For example, thinking that you might make a mistake. Once again, an incisive question such as 'If you knew that you would do a perfect job, what would you do first?' or 'If you knew that we would all experience valuable learning from any mistakes, how would you approach this differently?' can help someone to look beyond that possibility and open up their mind to new possibilities.

Finally, there are assumptions that run deeper that are linked to our beliefs about ourselves and our experience of the world. These will often haunt our thinking continually. For example, for years my belief that I wasn't good enough underpinned everything in my life. Because I felt I wasn't good enough I held back on trying all sorts of new things and I lived in my husbands' shadows for years. It was only years later, when a friend asked me how I'd like to develop my future after the break-up of my third marriage when I was at an all-time low, that I had a real breakthrough. I kept saying that if only I was good enough I would do this and do that, until finally she said to me, 'If you knew that you are good enough, what would you do

See IDEA 18, *Liberate your thinking*, for a couple of powerful examples of removing barriers.

Try another idea...

differently?' When I said I didn't know she immediately said, 'Well if you did know, what would it be?' Suddenly the floodgates opened and all the ideas that I'd stifled over the years came flooding out. It was an amazing experience.

THE POSITIVE PHILOSOPHICAL CHOICE

If we truly wish to help others or ourselves to think, feel and perform at their best, then perhaps we need to start from the viewpoint that everyone already has everything they need to achieve their potential. So adopting a positive philosophy of human nature would seem appropriate – choosing to accept that human beings are by nature good. That they're intelligent, kind, emotional, powerful, multi-talented, assertive, imaginative and logical.

'Obstacles are the things a person sees when he takes his eyes off the goal.'
E. JOSEPH COSSMAN,
US sales expert

Defining idea...

155

How did
it go?

Q **I've tried to remove my 'possible fact' assumption that if I apply for a promotion and don't get the job, I might make my present boss angry, which would make doing the same job very uncomfortable. I've thought it through, but at the last moment I keep coming back to that possibility. How do I overcome it and go for the job?**

A *Perhaps it would be helpful for me to ask you a question. If you knew that your boss could be encouraged to be supportive of your wish to develop your career, what would you do right now?*

Q **I'd really love to start my own business. But I could never get it off the ground, as I have no capital to invest. I have lots of good ideas, but I can't really see the point in dwelling on them because I obviously need money to live whilst the business is getting going. I understand what you've said, but this is a very real issue. How can I get going?**

A *I understand completely as I faced the same problem ten years ago. I had a vision, but I needed money to make it happen. This meant that I never really thought beyond a certain point. Then one day someone asked me the question, 'If money wasn't an issue, how would you go about setting your business up?' It freed my thinking to such a degree that I suddenly began to think of all sorts of opportunities to get some financial backing for my business and I put a real plan in place. It's been the most exciting time of my life.*

36

Learning from mistakes

We can choose to either learn from our mistakes when they happen or believe that we're just unlucky and go on to repeat the same errors.

Whether we view a challenge as a problem or an opportunity greatly affects the way that we deal with it.

FIND THE REPEATING PATTERNS

I was a slow learner. After my first failed marriage, you'd have thought that I'd have really looked at what went wrong. And after my second failing in a similar way, you'd definitely have thought that I'd look a little harder. To have it happen a third time quite obviously isn't a coincidence! Yet I wasn't learning anything from my experiences. I felt victimised, unlucky and very hard done by. It was only after reading *You Can Heal Your Life* by Louise Hay that I began to examine what was probably obvious to everyone else. She'd written something that seemed, at the time, to be utterly amazing. She'd cured herself of cancer by changing her thinking. She'd taken 100% responsibility for herself and her mistakes, something that at this point in my life I hadn't done at all. In my case, I'd encouraged men to treat me as

Here's an idea for you...

Find a quiet place and look back over your life and pinpoint any repeating patterns – some you may like and some you'll dislike. Now ask yourself what the belief is that's driving those experiences. Do it by asking, 'What was I assuming about myself in this circumstance?' Write down the first thoughts that enter your head. Then, for the unhelpful assumptions, ask another question by turning the negative belief into a positive. For example, when I was carrying the belief that I wasn't good enough I might have asked the question, 'If I knew that I am good enough what would I say right now, what would I do in this moment or where would I choose to go on holiday?'

though they knew best; they were the bosses and they made the big decisions.

I was only there to support and look after them and the family. They also controlled the money and so on. Moreover, I blamed them when they got it wrong!

NOW CHANGE THEM!

After reading *You Can Heal Your Life* I read countless other such book, and all the authors were saying similar things but from different perspectives. I then took a long hard look at

why I was creating these circumstances in my life and, for the first time, I really owned my mistakes. I began to realise that all of my experiences were actually giving me feedback about my internal world – the way I was thinking. I'd simply chosen not to listen. I now treat my mistakes as learning opportunities and ask myself how can I change me rather than how can I change other people. This was the turning point in my life and now I make sure I regularly ask myself what I really want.

Find someone who will support and listen to you while you're thinking through your experiences. Try IDEA 25, *When feelings hamper thinking*.

Try another idea...

'You are always free to change your mind and choose a different future, or a different past.'
RICHARD BACH, US author

Defining idea...

How did it go?

Q **Some of this makes perfect sense, but I'm uncomfortable with the question 'What do *I* really want?' Isn't this being horribly selfish?**

A *It depends on what your values are. I think it's far better to be clear and open about what you really want and what feels right for you. Have you ever chosen not to share what you really want and then felt resentful because your feelings weren't being considered? If your values are about loving and caring for others, you can still be really honest with yourself and with them and then agree a way forward that suits everyone.*

Q **Can there be repeating patterns in completely different areas of your life? I seem to be making similar mistakes in utterly different circumstances.**

A *Yes, definitely. After my three marriages I very nearly took my Personal Leadership Programme into someone else's business so that it became part of their portfolio. The boss wanted me to change the programme as he felt it wouldn't sell the way it was. I knew that the way that I'd designed it was best for the client, but the boss was much more powerful and knowledgeable than I was. I nearly gave in, but at the last moment I walked away. It was only when I looked back on my life that I realised this was an exact replica of what happened in my marriages. I allowed another man to convince me that he knew best! The programme, as I designed it, has now had over 9,000 people go through it – it did sell and is still selling!*

37

What else do I think about me?

Your beliefs about the roles that you are to play in life can lead you to places you really don't want to be.

When I look back at the beliefs I acquired as a child, I realise how much of a hold they had on me. Years later, I still find them jumping up and punching me on the nose.

THE LEAST USEFUL BELIEFS

I can clearly remember my Dad saying to me when I was a young teenager and not the least bit interested in cooking that I must be a good cook and always have dinner on the table for my husband otherwise my husband would leave me! I saw my wonderful stepmother as the perfect example of a good wife – the house was immaculate, there were always flowers around, meals were delicious and she made jam from our own fruit. There are also memories that aren't so great – having to sit for hours topping and tailing gooseberries, taking the stones out of cherries and de-stalking redcurrants and blackcurrants! I also remember that it was Dad who did

Here's an idea for you...

Pinpoint areas of your life where you feel under pressure. Where are you constantly trying to do too much and feel slightly resentful about the pressure you're under or the way others seem to have unrealistic expectations of you? Ask yourself why you're choosing to do these things and what you're assuming about your role in this. Then look back at the patterns in your life – where else have you seen the behaviours that you're now demonstrating? Are you entirely happy with this behaviour or is it something from the past that you'd now like to change? Make whatever choices are required for you to become more closely aligned with how you now think.

all the paperwork, paid all the bills and made decisions about major things that needed doing in the house. I grew up with the firm belief that women were there to support men and that men looked after the money! Logically, and in this day and age, this view really doesn't stack up, and intellectually it doesn't feel right for me. But does this childhood belief still influence me? Yes. All the time. Even now I find myself telling my partner to sit down while I do the washing up or trying to find the time to fit shopping and cooking into my crazy schedule. My partner's more or less retired and I work full time! I also find myself feeling guilty when I see all the apples on the tree and I haven't found the time to bottle them or turn them into jam.

THE MENTAL CONFLICT

At times like these I ask myself the question, 'What am I assuming?' The answer is nearly always the same, which suggests to me that some beliefs never really go away and can return just as strongly unless we remain constantly aware. My incessant beliefs are that I'm not good enough (I have to keep proving that I am good enough) and that a woman's role in life is to always be mother, mistress, wife and constant support. I have no wish to lose some of these beliefs because, for example, despite being a successful businesswoman, I still wish to retain my femininity. Some of my beliefs have changed; some have gone forever, such as the one about men always making the financial decisions. This particular belief has gone because I now have such strong evidence that, for me, this is an untruth.

Taking a look at your vision might help you to identify whether you're deliberately or unconsciously off track because some of your old beliefs are getting in the way. Take a look at IDEA 24, *Why plan your life?*

Try another idea...

'*Because you are in control of your life. Don't ever forget that. You are what you are because of the conscious and subconscious choices you have made.*'
BARBARA HALL, *A Summons to New Orleans*

Defining idea...

How did it go?

Q **I'm just like you and I grew up in a similar environment. Most of my friends still live that way and I feel guilty that I'm no longer enjoying it. The crazy thing is that my husband keeps telling me that he'd be perfectly happy for me to go out to work and do whatever makes me happy. How do I take the first step?**

A *I suspect that you may also have a belief that change is going to be incredibly difficult. Please do your vision before you do anything and then ask yourself, 'If I knew that this is going to be easy and fun, what might I do today as a first step?' Sit down and tell your husband that you do want to do things differently and tell him why you're having difficulties, that your beliefs are holding you back. Ask him for his support, and when you panic get him to ask you the question that I've just given you. Good luck. I did it, starting at the age of fifty, and so can you!*

Q **If you change the circumstances that you're in, doesn't that automatically change the belief?**

A *In my experience, no. I once believed that if I changed the circumstances then everything would be different, but the belief working in my inner world meant that I simply re-created the same thing again – my three almost identical marriages. Really look for where you have repeating patterns that you're not happy with and take some time to go somewhere quietly and question yourself. Why are you creating these situations? What do you believe is your role in this? What are your beliefs about life, marriage, working women, men? You'll soon uncover some interesting beliefs that you carry.*

38

Love is a choice

When we fall head over heels in love it's easy to believe that this wonderful, euphoric feeling will last forever. As everyday life takes over, however, this feeling gets pushed aside.

We're then inclined to think that love is fading or that it's disappeared completely. We're left wishing it could return and can feel deprived if it doesn't. Love is a verb, however, not simply an emotion.

TAKE CHARGE OF YOUR FEELINGS

When I was married, my poor husbands didn't have a chance. I expected life to continue in the romantic way that it had before we got married and I expected them to continue to do all the wonderful romantic things that they'd done before. How I expected this to happen once we were both working and there were six children to look after really didn't come into the equation. Even more fascinating when I look back is that I expected them to know this and to know what to do because I believed it was their role in life to make me feel loved.

Here's an idea for you... **Look at the list of things that you'd like your partner to do for you. Then do what you can off that list for them! See what happens and after a few days ask your partner how they feel when you do those things. Explain lovingly how much value you place on your relationship and that it would be even more wonderful if they could reciprocate. Choose to do these things regardless of how you feel and not just when you feel loving, which would be easy. Remember that loving is a verb, not just an emotion. Doing loving things when you don't 'feel' loving is the act of a strong and committed person.**

For me to feel loved I needed them to tell me frequently that they loved me, bring me flowers, remember all the things that I liked, hold my hand whenever we were out, look lovingly at me, remember anniversaries, bring me surprise little gifts, cuddle me at every available opportunity – the list was endless. If they didn't do all these things then I wouldn't feel loved and I would blame *them*. This was scary stuff when I began to really think about it for I was completely giving away my power. I wasn't taking responsibility one iota. I was effectively saying to them that it was up to them to make me feel loved and that if they didn't do their job I could blame them.

I don't mind telling you that this was one of the most difficult things for me to grasp, but now I don't need any of these things. I can choose to feel loved in each and every moment. I can feel loved doing the washing up, I can feel loved when I pick up the phone to one of my children and tell them how much I love them and I can feel loved speaking to a group of a thousand people.

CHOOSING LOVE IS THE MOST USEFUL OPTION

Compile a list of all the things that your partner has to do for you to feel really loved by them. If it helps, list all the things that they do that make you feel unloved and then turn them into their positive opposites. Ask yourself how likely it is that anyone can do everything on your list for you. Then ask yourself who's really responsible for how you feel. You might thing that other people are, yet who chooses your thoughts? You do. So why not change your thoughts? By all means share with your partner what value you place on yourself and, therefore, how you'd like to be treated because you think you deserve it, but then keep your power for you. The minute you tell someone that it's up to them to make you happy or feel loved, you've handed your power to them and lost control. How useful is that? Commit to thinking of one thing each morning that you could do for yourself that day to help you feel more loved and more loving towards yourself and to others. And do it!

You can change a relationship simply by focusing on what you can *give* to it rather than what you can get from it. See IDEA 1, *What you are is what you get.*

Try another idea...

'To love deeply in one direction makes us more loving in all others.'
ANNE-SOPHIE SWETCHINE, *Russian mystic*

Defining idea...

How did it go?

Q **I found this really difficult as most of the time I feel I don't count. However, I wrote a list of the ways that I'd like my husband to treat me and when I looked hard at what I'd written I felt very uncomfortable because I realised that I did hardly any of those things for him, even though I used to. When I started to do some of those things for him he became more loving towards me after the initial shock. But is it possible to keep this up? And doesn't it become artificial?**

A *Why on earth would you want to stop doing something that's working!? Life can, however, take over and the urgent becomes more important than the truly important, but take responsibility for keeping it up. You and your partner could decide to do whatever it takes to remind yourselves to keep it up, such as sticking a note on your fridge or headboard or setting an alarm on your computer. You could also ask your children to help and turn it into a love game – see who can do the most caring and loving things each day.*

Q **Are you really saying that changing your thoughts is this easy?**

A *No, absolutely not. I wish it were easy, for the world would be a happier and more loving place. The first step is to recognise that you have the opportunity to change how you feel about you and your life. The second step is to totally own that opportunity, to take 100% responsibility for you and be determined to hang on to that through thick and thin. It will only take a few days before you start to see positive changes and seeing that this process works will make it easier and easier to raise your level of commitment.*

39

Be careful how you say it

Communication isn't as easy as we might think as words mean different things to different people. When we want to disagree with someone we need to focus on the outcome that we'd ideally like.

Disagreement is healthy. Constructive criticism is useful. Unless we can challenge other people's thinking, we may never come up with creative ideas.

THE WHY AND THE HOW

We can have a different opinion from others for many varied reasons. For example, we may have more experience, more information, more instinct or more skill. It would be remarkable if we always agreed with other people's ideas. In some instances our opinion may be valid and in some instances it may not be, for example, where it's emotionally laden and based on unfortunate experiences. But is it right and sensible to express our opinions? Of course it is. How useful is it if we're part of a meeting or discussion and don't say what we think or feel?

Here's an idea for you...

Choose a situation involving you and someone else where you've got it wrong and there's bad feeling surrounding an idea that's being explored. Apologise, even if you don't think it's your fault, and say that you'd like to re-evaluate some of that thinking. Put aside your feelings about them and focus on their idea. Keep listening and do your best to understand them. Ask questions to clarify things and to learn about the experiences they've had that are causing them to make their suggestion. Be sure that any disagreement is about the idea, not the individual. Continue until things are resolved or you at least have a clearer understanding of why they're so keen on their suggestion. Remember to thank them for a useful session.

For example, imagine that you're discussing with your family where to go on holiday, and everyone is plumping for a particular place in France. You happen to know, as a result of what you've been reading in the newspapers, that there's a huge conference going on in that particular place in that particular month. Unless you disagree and share that information, you're likely to find your holiday destination absolutely packed with businesspeople, with traffic a nightmare and the noise at night unbearable because all the nightclubs will be swinging until the early hours. So, disagreeing can be useful and necessary.

It's how you do it is that counts. The knack is to stay focused on the subject. So, in this example a useful and constructive way to disagree with the place chosen for the holiday would be, 'Love the sound of France because it fulfils so many of our requirements, but I'd be most unhappy with the place because…'. However, suppose you said something along the lines of, 'Why do you always come up with these stupid ideas? Haven't you read the papers recently? Don't you know that this big conference is happening at this time? You really are daft.' You've lost focus on the subject and you're focusing on the individual instead. And what's the likely response? 'Who are you saying is daft? What about that article you missed in the paper recently and how you made an idiot of us both in front of my boss at that cocktail party we went to!?' The person has become defensive as a result of your attack on them as a person and, therefore, felt the need to come back at you. Nothing has been achieved.

Look at IDEA 23, *Talk in their terms*, or IDEA 47, *Egg timer peace*, to remind you about the importance of trying to understand where people are coming from before attempting to drive your ideas through.

Try another idea...

HOW USEFUL IS THAT?

I see this happen so often, both at work and at home. When people feel that their value as a human being and as a contributor is being threatened they go straight for the jugular and seem to think that this will have a useful outcome. Nobody likes being attacked as a person. If you verbally attack someone else they're likely to respond in one of two ways. They'll either withdraw completely and contribute nothing more, perhaps trying to sabotage the idea or agreed action later, or they'll come back with a hard and fast response. However, challenging someone's ideas in the right way, especially if their good ideas are listened to and supported, is entirely useful and they'll soon learn that this is constructive and helpful. It's likely to encourage them to respond in the same way and new thinking can emerge as a result.

'It is better to debate a question without settling it than to settle a question without debating it.'
JOSEPH JOUBERT,
French philosopher

Defining idea...

171

How did
it go?

Q **One of my colleagues goes for anyone who doesn't agree with her. Even her boss seems out of his depth and doesn't know how to deal with it, especially as she's very powerful and articulate. Can you help me cope with her?**

A *I can feel the hairs on the back of my neck stand up as I read this, for this was my last husband to a T! You could ask your colleague how well her ideas are being received and how supportive people are of her suggestions. In my experience it's unlikely that this behaviour encourages anything other than greater conflict. Suggest that you may be able to find a way of getting her ideas accepted and supported in a far more positive way. Then get her to read this idea! Help her focus on the outcome that she'd really like, not just on a browbeaten acceptance of her and her ideas.*

Q **My partner does this to me all the time and I get really nasty back. We seem always to be rowing. How can I break the pattern?**

A *You're right in that it is just a case of breaking the pattern. At the moment you're in an unbroken circle: he says something nasty, you respond, he says something nastier, you respond, and so on. Break the pattern by responding in a different way. You could ask him if there's anything else he thinks or feels about the matter and then say something positive back, or apologise for putting him down and say that you'd rather get back to the topic, or tell him that you understand that's how he thinks and feels but that you see it slightly differently. Remember that no one can make you angry or upset unless you give them permission. The power is with you.*

40

Laughter is the best medicine

We choose how we think and don't have to be driven by our emotions.

Recognising that we can choose to be happy whenever we want is unbelievably empowering.

I used to spend much of my life stressed and unhappy, always worrying about tomorrow and about things that I had or hadn't done yesterday.

HAPPINESS IS A CHOICE

So says the author and speaker Robert Holden and, guess what, he's right! When I first started on my path of real growth I had to do some very deep soul-searching. One of the things that I needed to ask was why I felt stressed or depressed so often. The answer became clear. It was because I was choosing to feel that way. After all, I choose my thoughts, no one else does. I couldn't walk away from this fact, however hard it was for me to accept it.

Here's an idea for you...

Think of a chore that you really don't like doing. It might be similar to one of my daily tasks that really isn't great – I have seven dogs, and every day there's a little garden job called 'poo patrol'! Now decide how you're going to feel about doing this job. You can focus on how great the garden will look when you've finished and how happy that'll make you. Or you could focus on the great joy and happiness that the dogs bring into you life. Whatever chore you pick, choose to be happy during each moment that you're doing it.

At this precise moment, I'm sitting here writing this book to a very tight deadline. The sun is shining outside, I'm exhausted from a ridiculous work schedule and my hot tub is calling me. It may not be easy for me to choose to be happy at this moment, and if I don't choose to be happy it'll be much harder and take much longer for me to write this chapter. I'm choosing happiness!

I clearly remember a friend and colleague phoning me to tell me how excited she was about a new job she'd just been offered in Brussels. She was beside herself with joy and then told me that she'd be really happy once she was out there and had left her present job. I asked her why she was choosing to put off happiness until she got to Brussels instead of having a little happiness right now. She went very quiet and then said, 'I've never thought about things in that way. You're right, I can choose to be happy right now, and I am.'

How many people do you know who say that they'll be happy once they get their new car, new job or new home? But what happens when they get that new car? They love it for a while, but as soon as they get bored with it and a faster, flashier model comes out they're once again saying, 'I'll be happy once I get that new car!' What they're doing is putting happiness outside of them, in an object of some sort. But that's not where happiness lies. Happiness lies inside of us and all it takes to be happy is for us to choose to be so.

Look at IDEA 1, _Who you are is what you get_, to refresh your memory of the joy we get from giving to others.

Try another idea...

WHAT'S YOUR CHOICE?

When you're at home, do you look out of the window and see a wonderful view? Or do you see the dirty windows? If you walk into someone else's home do you notice the beautiful paintings on the walls or do you see the untidiness in the room? You need to make a choice about what you're going to focus on. It probably won't be so easy to be a happy person if you always look for the negative rather than the positive. Remember that if we continually say, 'I'll be happy when...' we're actually choosing to while away our life in a state of 'unhappiness' until we reach this destination called 'happiness'. However, once we truly own our thoughts and the way we feel, we can choose happiness in whatever we do.

'Most people are as happy as they make up their minds to be.'
ABRAHAM LINCOLN

Defining idea...

How did it go?

Q   **I can't believe that you can be happy all of the time. What about when your son died? However did you cope with that?**

A   *Of course I wasn't happy during that time. I was in shock and devastated and at times I even felt that my life was over. However, I allowed myself time to grieve and then I consciously started to do things and tell myself that during those moments I was happy, such as walking my dogs around Virginia Water Lake. Day by day I became aware of more moments of happiness. And that was how I built myself back up again. I knew that unless I did this I'd be of no value to me or my other children.*

Q   **I realised when I read this that I put happiness outside of me nearly all the time. I can find it in my job, my car, my relationship if it's going well and when people are nice to me. How easy will it be for me to turn this around?**

A   *Initially I found it hard. I kept forgetting! But once I became aware that it was usually when I recalled something in the past or worried about what might happen in the future that I became unhappy, the thing that helped me more than anything else was consciously living in the present moment. I literally kept having to draw my attention back to how I felt in the present moment, but when I did it was nearly always easy to feel happy.*

41

Every day counts

Every day we're presented with the opportunity to have a new beginning and say, 'Today I can choose how I think and feel in each and every moment.'

What do you focus on each day? What do you look for? Do you choose to complain about things? Or do you rejoice in all the wonderful things that you have in your life?

BE CAREFUL WHAT YOU LOOK FOR AS YOU MIGHT JUST FIND IT!

For most of my life I got frustrated about something on a daily basis. For example, dreadful traffic making me late for an appointment, the hairdresser cutting my hair badly, my husband never buying me flowers, the children making a filthy mess in the house and leaving me to clear it up, losing a sale that I should have got or my best friend not supporting me when I moaned about my lot in life! When I look back, I find it quite pathetic how easy I found it to look at my life and see problems everywhere. The sad thing was that I didn't see or appreciate the many, many things that I did have. If, even at the most challenging times in my life, someone

Here's an idea for you... **Commit to doing the following exercise each night. List sixty things to be grateful for that day. This might seem like an impossible target, but try it anyway. You could gradually build up the numbers – ten things on the first evening, fifteen on the second day, and so on. Also, you might start to think of things earlier in the day or even first thing in the morning. Interestingly, there will be a gradual change in your focus and you may even find that the more you focus on good things, the more good things appear.**

had asked me to write down the things that I really did appreciate I could have listed my six wonderful children, my great health and energy, having lots of wonderful friends, having a roof over my head and earning enough money to pay for it, eating well and never going hungry, having had some wonderful life experiences, having a car that carries me safely from A to B, having people who love me, having clients who rate me, making a positive difference to many people's lives in a small way, never being lonely, having the chance to try many different things. The list would have been endless, but instead I took all these things for granted.

How often do you look at each day as a blessing? How often do you appreciate the fact that you've actually woken up and are in this world to enjoy another day! How much of life do we actually assume is ours by right, without any thought of what wonderful opportunities we actually have? When I wouldn't eat my lunch I can remember my parents saying to me, 'Now eat it up. Think of all the starving people in Africa.' I had absolutely no concept of what they were talking about. I can just remember thinking, 'Well they can have it!'

SO WHERE IS YOUR ATTENTION?

What do you focus on and how useful is it? When I began to realise what I focused on I made a huge effort to change my thinking. I knew that I wasn't living my life as though each day was important. I don't think I was even consciously living it – I just got on with each day without even thinking of the blessings that were there for me in each moment. Let me share with you something that I once heard, 'What you put your attention on expands; what you take your attention away from withers and dies.' I can't remember where I heard it, but it could have been from Wayne Dyer, who I consider one of the greatest personal development gurus. If you focus on the good things in life then you'll see more of them in every day.

How can you help your family, friends and colleagues begin to think positively? See IDEA 10, *It's a team game.*

Try another idea...

'*I am still determined to be cheerful and happy, in whatever situation I may be; for I have also learned from experience that the greater part of our happiness or misery depends upon our dispositions and not upon our circumstances.*'
MARTHA WASHINGTON, first First Lady

Defining idea...

181

How did it go?

Q **How can you possibly look at all the positive things when your life is a mess from start to finish?**

A *The first thing to recognise is that you've almost certainly been thinking like that for a long time so you're constantly focusing on what's wrong. You're then likely to be creating more and more of what you're focusing on. Put simply, shift your focus and each and every day appreciate one or two positive things about your day. Then increase this number to four, and so on. Try the exercise recommended above – just go for it and let me know what happens! After I left my last husband my life was a complete disaster zone too – no man, no money only debt so nothing to pay the bills with, the death of my second son, no confidence, no marketable skills that I could see, no training in anything. I managed to change my way of thinking, and so can you.*

Q **I find it really difficult just living in today. I'm always worrying about what's going to happen tomorrow. I tell myself that this makes me more effective as I'm an inveterate planner. Are you saying that I should plan less?**

A *Not necessarily, but get the balance right. If you're constantly focusing on the future then that, in fact, is where you are. Remember, the most valuable commodity you have is time. Do you really want to live your life always giving that commodity away? The more you can live in the present, which is where your power is, the more you can create change. You can't create change in the future or the past.*

42

Are we all leaders?

Whatever the role – boss, friend, parent or colleague – the minute that you're in a position where you can influence another person you are, in fact, leading.

I believe the mark of outstanding leadership is not just how good a leader you are, but how many leaders you develop. Many are good at the former but, in my experience, few are good at the latter.

STRIVING FOR A BALANCED COMPANY

What do we need to consider if we want a high-performing organisation? We need a balance between two things. First we need to have a clear vision about what we're here for, where we want to go, what our product is, what markets we want to sell in, what profit we intend to make, what culture we aspire to, how we wish to be perceived, the strategy that will get us there, the structure and systems to support the strategy, and so on. On the flip side of the coin, we need people with the right experience, skills and knowledge and the right energy, commitment and attitude. To get the balance right almost requires a negotiation. The individuals are asking for

Stop telling your children what to do. Ask them what they really want then get them to tell you what they think the benefits and risks of this are. If they don't want to do their homework, ask them what the consequences will be if they don't and the benefits if they do? Then ask whether they're prepared to take 100% responsibility for the outcome of whatever they choose to do. Leave them to decide. If they choose not to do the homework and they complain about the unpleasant outcome the next day, smile and tell them that they made a conscious choice and ask them what they've learned from it.

enough information, resources, support and freedom to go out and deliver, and the organisation is agreeing but needs to ensure that it has the right measurements in place to know that they're doing that which it requires, selling the right products at the right price, doing the hours necessary, and so on. It's virtually impossible not to have a high-performing organisation if the right balance is achieved.

However, how often is this balance actually achieved? Sometimes it goes more the way of the individual, but more often it swings towards the organisation. Think of a company that employs great people who have the freedom to make lots of money for the company and are consistently very successful. Unfortunately, when they hit a problem the systems aren't robust enough to pick it up quickly. I'm sure you've heard of a bank called Barings! Now imagine the other extreme. An organisation is going through tough times so it tightens its belt and makes people redundant. It also restructures and sharpens its systems and believes that these new initiatives will cause people to behave differently. Sadly, the reality is that people feel nervous and threatened, they're not sure about the new way of working and because they know that they could get it wrong and be fired, they try to continue to do things the way they did before. Plenty of companies that make these changes end up wondering why they're only partly successful.

LEADERSHIP IN THE HOME

Isn't this the same at home? With our children, aren't we constantly trying to get the balance right between rules and freedom? Don't we do our best to get the 'systems' and 'structure' in place to make the family unit work effectively? Think about what we're likely to do when the pressure is on, such as when the children aren't doing their homework or they're getting home later and later on schoolnights. We keep having to set new 'rules' and 'regulations'. How successful are they? Probably less successful than we'd like them to be so we end up having to create more and more rules.

So how can we deal with this? We get people to fundamentally change the way they think and to understand responsibility. Imagine a child says that they can't do well at maths because the teacher is lousy. If she were taking 100% responsibility for maths then it wouldn't matter whether she had a good or bad teacher. She'd find a way to study the subject despite her current teacher.

To be a leader who develops others we need to change how we communicate. We need to stand back from advice and start asking people how they'd deal with their own issues. We need to get people to take 100% responsibility for their own life. So to help people change, we need to change first.

Understanding more about the power of communication may help to get people to take more responsibility. See IDEA 16, *Please let me think*.

Try another idea...

'*A leader is someone who can take people to a place they don't think they can go.*'
BOB EATON

Defining idea...

How did it go?

Q **I now realise that my leadership beliefs were about telling people what to do and then inspiring them. Your first comment struck home – I'm good at leading but I know how much things slip when I'm not around. Is there a quick way to get people to take responsibility?**

A *It can be quick, but only if you can communicate to people what responsibility means, why it's important and how it benefits them. When you've got everyone together take the opportunity to explain to them what you think is the role of a leader. Then ask what you could do to enable them to become more effective leaders. Give them the responsibility of telling you what they need. Then follow their recommendations because they'll own the solution.*

Q **My child seems incapable of knowing what's best for him. It would be a disaster if I stopped telling him what to do! How can I deal with him?**

A *I suggest you let him do whatever he needs to do. If he messes things up he'll learn from that, especially if you help him think through the messy outcome, without giving advice. I used to solve all my children's problems and as a result they were still coming to me as young adults asking me to solve their problems. But what would they do if I'm not around? I was silly not to develop them and it's taking me quite some time to re-educate them. What's worse is that despite everything that I now know and teach I'm still tempted to fall into the same trap!*

43

How we view the world

External influences condition our thinking and create subconscious beliefs that can affect how we react to people and situations. We need to be aware of our conditioning and beliefs in order to achieve top-quality thinking.

External influences come from many sources, including our families, teachers, friends, religion, governments and the media. In fact, anyone and every situation we face.

STIMULUS AND RESPONSE

What would you think of someone who went to a public school? There could be various responses to this question from very positive ones, such as 'well-educated', 'well-mannered' or 'a logical thinker', to less positive ones, such as 'posh', 'snobbish' or 'arrogant'. Generally, most people have a combination of the two types of response. These responses reflect the fact that we've built our own stereotype of a person who went to a public school, which means that we run the terrible danger of operating from that conditioning when we come into contact with such a person, to the extent that we could be discriminating against them.

Look for conditioning in your own attitudes. Be aware of what you think of a person when you meet them for the first time. Think, perhaps, of someone for whom you have scant regard. There might be some conditioning affecting your opinion of them. Conditioning often stops us from really hearing what a person is saying, as we filter their words through our prejudice. Next time you meet this person listen hard to what they're saying – you may be surprised by how much more you learn about them.

I came across a perfect example of this discriminating behaviour on one of my courses. A man had a solid belief about qualifications. To hear him speak you'd think that anyone without qualifications didn't work hard enough, wasn't intelligent and wasn't interested in improving themselves. He was completely closed to hearing different opinions in this respect. At the end of the three-day programme, I asked him how he'd found the course. He said, 'Incredible, probably one of the best programmes I've done. I've learned so much from it, it's cleared up a lot of misunderstandings and I'm already a better leader as a result.' I told him that I was delighted and then asked how he'd feel if I told him I had no qualifications whatsoever. He said that he wouldn't believe me. I told him that it was true and that I'd nearly been thrown out of every school I went to. I told him that I might have done some things since but that I had no qualifications in his sense of the word. At that point, he had to question the belief that had been at the heart of his thinking for many years. He then admitted that he couldn't possibly look me in the eye and say that I wasn't intelligent and didn't want to learn. That I was unqualified completely blew his belief out of the window.

THE POTENTIAL DANGERS OF CONDITIONING

How many people had that man disadvantaged in his work and social life? How many rich experiences had he missed out on by writing off people without qualifications? Beliefs can have a huge impact unless we begin to recognise them and challenge them. You may not have a problem in this regard, but think about the people around you. For example, check how many of your male colleagues are limiting the potential of their female colleagues by conditioning that's led them to such beliefs as: men are better than women; women are only really interested in running a home and having babies; the minute a problem crops up, women will stay at home and let the team down; women aren't as strong as men so men need to make the big decisions; men mustn't expect too much from women; men can pretend to listen to women but really men know best.

My beliefs about me – I'm not good enough; it's my role in life to support my man; the man handles the finances so I give him all the money; ultimately the man makes the major decisions; I stay at home while the man goes out and earns the money; if the man is unhappy it must be my fault – held me back for years. There are too many to mention here. And I probably haven't uncovered them all!

IDEA 35, *We are what we decide to be*, looks at freeing ourselves of some of the conditioning and beliefs that limit our aspirations.

Try another idea...

'**How things look on the outside of us depends on how things are on the inside of us.**'
PARK COUSINS

Defining idea...

189

How did it go?

Q **I enjoy sport and although my wife thinks that I'm quite a sensitive man she's convinced that the men I play sport with are male chauvinists and refuses to have anything to do with them. This means that I can never persuade her to come along to any of the social events at my sports club. How can I persuade her otherwise?**

A *It sounds as if your wife has come across some chauvinistic sportsmen in the past and has become convinced that they're all the same. Perhaps you could arrange a social event with your sports friends somewhere other than the sports club and with some other friends as well so that she can meet them in an environment that seems less threatening to her.*

Q **I run a presentation course for senior managers. One of the issues I raise with them individually is what they think their appearance says about them. I do this to check that they're presenting an image they think is appropriate. I haven't raised this issue with women since two of them regarded it as personal and became upset. Is this their conditioning or mine?**

A *It's probably their conditioning. They may have experienced men hinting that it's appearance that counts if you're a woman in a man's world. Perhaps it would help if you told them that you also raise this issue with men, and providing an example of how it's helped their colleagues might soften their conditioning.*

44

How do I persuade them?

**We all want to steer people towards our way of thinking.
So, what's the most effective way of influencing people?**

When we want people to follow our lead, we usually try to find as many different ways to get our thoughts across as possible. If someone disagrees, we just try to come at it another way. However, does this actually work?

A PICTURE

Picture a pile of sand. If I pour a jug of water over the sand it's likely that some of it will be soaked up by the sand and that some of it will trickle down the edge of the pile making pathways as it goes. If I pour another jug of water on the same pile of sand, more may soak in and some may make new pathways. Most of it, however, is likely to travel down the original pathways and make these deeper. If I pour yet another jug of water over the sand it will be virtually impossible for the water to do anything other than go down the existing pathways, making them deeper than ever.

For the duration of your very next conversation try not to use the word 'I' – I think, I suggest, I don't agree. Concentrate entirely on 'you'. Ask 'you' questions. What do you think about this? How might you handle this? Let me test what you are saying to be sure that I've understood you correctly. That is a great idea that you have just had. This way you'll see how much more people are able to contribute. You'll also notice how difficult you'll find it to not take over and voice your ideas.

This is almost exactly how the brain works. When you give someone a problem to solve they'll begin to think it through and pathways or traces will be created through the brain. You tell them you think they've got it wrong and they need to think it through again. This they do and they may possibly find a new pathway but it's highly likely that they'll go down the same pathway, making that idea deeper or more firmly entrenched. Ask them to think it through again and it'll be almost impossible for them to come up with a new solution. It's not that they don't want to, it's just that the pathways have now been created and the brain finds it virtually impossible to move away from those pathways.

When you look at this picture it's obvious that continually trying to change someone's mind by telling them, yet again, why you think the way you do, is likely to be less than useless.

'I' VERSUS 'YOU'

When we run our Personal Leadership Programme one of the first things that we do is measure how well people communicate. We all have a perception of the way we communicate and most of us think that we're open to ideas, that we show caring to others and that we encourage others to come forward with their thoughts and suggestions. People are typically shocked and horrified by the results of the measurement. We absolutely do not communicate the way we think we do. I've as yet found almost no exception to this.

Without even realising it, we usually communicate by giving our point of view, giving our suggestions and telling people why we don't agree with their ideas. What we don't do is support their ideas, ask for their opinions, test our understanding of what they're saying, summarise all their points of view, or take their ideas and demonstrate their value by building on them. We don't invite them into the conversation. In the first way, all our focus is on 'I'; in the second, it's all on 'you'. The thing I've discovered is that those of us in what you might describe as the caring professions are frequently the worst! Why? I suspect because we feel that we really need to give people the benefit of our wisdom.

Actually, if you really want to influence people the knack is to ask questions that allow them the opportunity to think abut something in a different way. In other words, allow the brain to come from a different start point. First, focus on helping them explore their idea. Then focus on developing their idea to incorporate ours.

> **For more on extending and building on other people's ideas have a look at IDEA 15, *Whose idea is it anyway?***

Try another idea...

> **'To listen well is as powerful a means of communication and influence as to talk well.'**
> JOHN MARSHALL

Defining idea...

195

How did
it go?

Q **I tried the exercise you suggested and found it very difficult. 'I' was creeping in all over the place and yet I really believe that I encourage others. Is there any way to make this easier?**

A *Unfortunately not. There are so many reasons why most of us end up communicating in this way and a lot of these appear to be good reasons. You now want to change lifetime habits. What I do suggest you do is ask the people closest to you – at home and work – to give you feedback on how you're coming across. Ask them to tell you honestly whether you're asking for their opinions, listening to them, supporting their ideas, and so on.*

Q **I'm trying to do this and getting lots of strange looks from my team. This is almost putting me off to the point where I'm tempted to revert. How can I handle this?**

A *If you suddenly change your behaviour it's not surprising that they may be confused. They may also mistrust what's going on. Under these circumstances I invariably give the same advice – label it! By that I mean explain what you're doing and why – because it makes sense to you and will help you become more effective as a leader. If you tell them that you need help in doing this they're almost certain to support you. Remember that you can't develop other leaders by telling them what to do all the time.*

45

No more indecision

**We don't often ask ourselves who we really want to be.
Yet, this is fundamental to how we live our lives.**

If you were no longer here, what would you want people to say about you? How would you like people to think about you? If you could be listening at the keyhole, what would you like to hear?

HOW DO YOU WANT TO BE REMEMBERED?

A good friend asked me these questions about ten years ago and gave me an exercise to do that was probably one of the most uncomfortable and most life-changing exercises that I've ever done. She asked me to write my obituary! In two steps. The first step was to think of the person that knew me the best, and write my obituary as though I'd just died and that person was writing it. I did this, imagining what Hazel might say. It contained many good things – how loving I was, what a caring and supportive friend and mother I was – and I felt proud to read these. However, there were some serious negatives that I didn't like writing or reading, including never fulfilling her potential, never being strong enough to stand up for

Here's an idea for you...

Write your own obituary and then pick one of the values that this has highlighted. For example, take 'Living your life with integrity'. Now list all the behaviours that you'll be demonstrating that will allow anybody you meet to say that you're a person with integrity. It may be things such as always telling the truth even when difficult, doing things that you say you're going to do, only agreeing to do something for someone else if you know you're not going to let them down, only talking about people to their faces and not gossiping behind their back, always dealing with issues that need to be dealt with, not blaming others for your mistakes, and so on. Do this with each of your values because unless you're clear about what behaviours support your stated values then nothing is likely to change.

what was right for her, putting husbands first and then blaming them when it all fell apart, never being really clear about what she wanted in life, and an awful lot more. I then asked Hazel to read it and she said that it was pretty accurate. Oh dear! This was not how I wanted to be remembered at all, so I knew I needed to do something about it.

Step two was to write some more obituaries as though I died at a wonderful age – at least ninety-five! I wrote four, from the point of view of one of my children, a loving partner, a business colleague and a special friend. These included very different things from those I'd written previously, such as 'As a mother she was a living example of how I want to be – she always encouraged me to be who I am, even if sometimes it wasn't what she would have wished...', 'As a business colleague she was always there for me and I could trust her with my deepest secrets knowing they would go no further...' and 'As a partner she always listened to me and loved me unconditionally...'.

Make sure you keep asking for feedback on how you're doing. Try IDEA 27, *Tell me how I'm doing.*

 Try another idea...

SO WHAT NOW?

When I looked at the difference between my first and second steps it became apparent that I wasn't being the person that I wanted to be. A whole lot of my values had become muddied. Did I really love unconditionally? Was I really allowing my children to fulfil their dreams or was I trying to make them how I wanted them to be? Was I really living my life with integrity? The answers made me fundamentally shift my values from my unconscious mind to the conscious. I became fully aware of how I wanted to be and totally committed to getting there. I still have that exercise and I look back at it occasionally to see how very far I have come.

'Knowing others is intelligence; knowing yourself is wisdom.'
LAO TZU

Defining idea...

How did it go?

Q   This sounded gruesome! However, it was quite the opposite. It liberated me, for I could see clearly who I really wanted to be and although the gap is quite big, I'll only need to take lots of little steps to make a difference. Is this usual?

A   *Definitely. Often when we look at where we are and how we need to change it seems too big a task because we look at the whole picture, which can be daunting. If you have an elephant in front of you and only a knife and fork, how might you eat it? A bite at a time! You only need to take little steps in order to make a huge difference in your life. If you've already tried appreciating people more than you criticise them, you'll already know this to be true.*

Q   I found the exercise really useful. However, I found listing the behaviours that match the values much more difficult. Is there an easy way to do this?

A   *Think of someone that you really admire. It doesn't need to be someone you know directly, it may be someone that you've read about or someone in the public eye. What is it about them that you admire and what is it that they actually do to demonstrate what you admire about them. For example, take Christopher Reeve, the Superman actor who is severely paralysed. It's pretty clear that one of his values is to 'make a difference', and behaviour that indicates this includes his ceaseless work for charity to raise money for research. He also stretches himself to be in the public eye, which he hates, so he can keep raising money and inspiring other paralysed people.*

46

No, no and no

Learning to say 'no' in an acceptable way, without being defiant, is a skill that we really need to develop.

I went through much of my life saying 'yes' to everyone, putting myself under a lot of pressure and then blaming them when I became exhausted!

SAYING 'NO' IS A GROWTH OPPORTUNITY

We all seem to be scared of saying 'no' to people – bosses, friends, colleagues, partners and sometimes even our children. When I look back over my marriages I'm amazed at how often I said 'yes' while actually thinking 'no', sometimes where major decisions were involved. For example, my third husband had a wonderful idea for a new product. The cost would be substantial and the risk reasonably high because, in all honesty, we hadn't done the market research. It just sounded like a great idea, and he loved designing new things. We needed money so I agreed to substantially increase our mortgage. Mad! Doubly mad, as it was my money that bought the house in the first place. Did I want to do it? Not really, but my belief that men make the big decisions probably interfered. I went ahead and increased

Wait until one of your children or friends asks you to do something that you typically would say 'yes' to, but deep down you really don't want to do. Then say 'no'. Until you're more experienced at saying 'no' it may be useful to provide an accompanying explanation, but learning how to say 'no' firmly, without the need to explain, is where you need to be heading.

the mortgage, the product didn't do as well as we thought it would and I ended up some years later with nothing.

In many ways, it was even worse when we needed to discuss what we were going to do when my children (his stepchildren) misbehaved. He could convince me, articulately and logically, to do all the things that he felt we should do. He was such a brilliant communicator and I never seemed to be able to be rational enough to argue my case. I didn't have the courage to say, 'No, I'm not doing it that way, even if I can't explain why.' So, even though I disagreed with something I would go along with it. After a while I'd be so uncomfortable with what we'd agreed that I'd do something different, which resulted in big rows! And he was in the right because I'd agreed to do it his way. And all this because I didn't know how to say 'no' in the first place.

It sometimes takes courage to be true to yourself and to ask, 'Is this really right for me at this time? How do I really think and feel about this?' Nevertheless, if we're going to take control of our lives, it's essential that we learn to say 'no'.

WORK–LIFE BALANCE

I meet so many people in the workplace who are totally stressed and feel out of control, overworked and undervalued. This is often because they haven't learned to say 'no'.

Understanding truly who you want to be may help you to be even more focused on what's right for you. Try IDEA 45, *No more indecision.*

Try another idea...

Instead they're taking on everything their boss, colleagues and staff are asking of them, then wondering why they're getting home later and later. You can imagine the scenario can't you, 'Oh Penny, I've got to dash out to this meeting and I haven't had time to finish typing that report. Could you do it for me please?' or 'Can you help me with this project please?' or 'Can you work late tonight to answer the phones?' or 'The slides haven't been done for tomorrow's session and we know how good you are at doing this. Could you please...?', and so on.

The knack is being able to say 'no' without offending anyone. If you have colleagues who continually dump stuff on you, then show them your list of priorities that have to be completed. Then ask them to choose which one you'd like their work to replace. Explain that if it's for another person or department they'll need to go to that person and tell them that the work you're currently doing will have to wait. They'll probably then take their work elsewhere. With your boss, you can do a similar thing, and more easily because all the stuff you're doing is likely to be for her.

'*We must become the change we want to see.*'
MAHATMA GANDHI

Defining idea...

How did it go?

Q **You make it sound so simple! But saying 'no' isn't just difficult; it's an art form! When I do say 'no' I end up feeling so guilty that I often reverse my decision. How do you stop the guilt?**

A *It isn't easy, and I regularly have to deal with the feeling you describe. My grown-up children occasionally ask me for financial help, which I could easily give them. However, sometimes this would be the wrong thing to do, so I say 'no'. I feel terrible afterwards and wonder how they'll cope without my help. However, deep down I know that I'm doing the best thing, for them as well as me. The more I leap in and help, the less I'm encouraging them to take responsibility for themselves and the more I'm stopping their growth. Try to understand that you're almost certainly doing the best thing for the other person when you say 'no'.*

Q **Why do you think we're so bad at this? At work I'm always being asked to do extra things and the more I say 'yes', the more people seem to ask things of me. I'm worried that if I change and start saying 'no', my job could be at risk. How do I take the first step?**

A *The best place to start is probably your boss. So, when your boss next asks you to do something, do what I suggested above and show them your list of the day's priorities and ask them which one they'd like you to defer until the next day. Be firm but pleasant and I'm sure you'll see a positive response.*

47

Egg timer peace

Developing an understanding of another person's viewpoint is the first step to resolving issues between you and other people.

Conflict can never be truly resolved unless both sides take the time to really understand the opposing viewpoint, which involves empathy. How many times have you been arguing with someone and suddenly said, 'Oh I didn't realise that's what you meant!'?

THE POWER OF THREE MINUTES

The only way to create this level of understanding is to stop focusing on our own point of view and start listening deeply to the other person. However, most of us find it very difficult to listen to someone else for any length of time without interrupting to agree or disagree or to add our own ideas, so I use an egg timer to help. I suggest that people take three minutes to explain how they feel while the others listen in silence. Then they swap over. This continues until they feel they

Here's an idea for you...

One of my husbands was a brilliant communicator and was consequently able to win all arguments by moving the goalposts. I often ended up defensive and in tears and feeling that I was in the wrong even though deep down I knew that I wasn't. I learned not to respond at all, but just to keep listening. I would then say, 'I'm really sorry that you see it that way but that isn't the way I see it.' However cross he got, that would be my response, for I knew that if I tried to get him to see it from my point of view – in other words, try to change him – I was on to a loser and would simply end up in a state. This approach worked every time and, boy, did it irritate him. I just removed myself from the argument – no more upset for me! Try it yourself.

both understand each other's situation and feelings. There's then a basis upon which to build a solution that suits everyone. Note that you're just listening to understand, not taking copious notes so you can come back and 'win the point'!

I've used this with many of my clients, including a large multinational chemical company where two divisions had major difficulties in dealing with each other. The root of the problem was that the two directors were at loggerheads and found it impossible to get along. I was asked to help and I arranged a meeting with both of them, in which I asked them to listen to each other in three-minute stretches. At the end of an hour and a half, they'd resolved all their differences and actually became friends. The egg timer worked well!

NOW I HEAR YOU

One of my clients asked me to run a programme for a group of young chief executives. The programme addressed issues that were consistent with both work and home life, and the delegates brought their wives and partners.

I wanted to demonstrate how effective the process of listening for three minutes each way was for resolving issues. I asked each couple to pick an issue from their personal lives that had so far remained unresolved. They carried out the exercise while I timed the three minutes and I asked them to observe the rules of allowing each person their time to talk without any interruptions and to genuinely listen. The entire exercise lasted forty-five minutes and by the time it concluded many people were in tears. Some were hugging each other; everyone was openly affectionate and supporting their partners.

One wife said that it was the first time she felt her partner had listened to her during their entire marriage – she had teenage children! One husband said that he'd never really understood the issue that his wife had talked about for months and that this had constantly caused a problem. Now he understood, they could now deal with the problem together – in fact, he said that it was already dealt with.

Try another idea...

If your partner comes home exhausted, put everything on hold and sit down and listen to her without interruption – however long it takes. IDEA 29, *But I asked you to listen to me*, shows more benefits of developing our listening skills, whether at home or at work.

Defining idea...

'*Seek first to understand, then to be understood.*'
STEVEN COVEY, leadership expert

How did it go?

Q I tried to listen to one of my team when we had an issue to deal with recently, but they weren't prepared to listen to me. Instead they kept interrupting when I was trying to explain my point of view. The discussion eventually dissolved into an argument because I got mad. How can I stop that from happening again?

A *It's hard when you first try new behaviours. However, if you really want others to understand you, then you have to be prepared to listen to them. It might help to explain the process before you start and say that you really want to understand their point of view, but that you'd also like to give your opinion. Then try using a clock or a watch to time each contribution.*

Q My wife says that I never listen to her and I have to admit that she's probably right, although I do try. This results in frequent misunderstandings, which can lead to arguments. How can I make myself listen more attentively?

A *Well done for admitting this. Listening is a learned skill and takes practice, but the first step is deciding that you want to listen better. Practise at every possible opportunity and begin to notice how much more you take in. Explain to your wife that you really want to be a better listener and ask her to help you by sitting down together to discuss things without other distractions.*

48

A problem or an opportunity?

How we view problems can make a big difference. We can either turn them into opportunities or into bigger problems.

Have you ever faced something that at the time seemed like a major problem, but later realised that without it you wouldn't be in the exciting place that you are today?

SO, WHICH IS IT?

I've faced some major problems in my life and I've treated some of them as an opportunity and some as the exact opposite. Let me give you two examples. The first example is when my last husband was having a relationship with a colleague that we were about to make a director of our company. It went way beyond just a business relationship. She admitted to me how much my husband had told her he cared for her and I threw a serious wobbly. I said that I didn't want her to become a director and that I wanted her to leave the company. My husband threatened to

Here's an idea for you... **Think of a problem then ask a question such as, 'If I knew that this situation is a real opportunity for me to learn or do something different with my life, how might I view this? What might I now do differently?' For comfort look back at your life and recall things that felt like disasters before you turned them into positives. Remember that life truly is what you make it.**

leave himself, which would have left me to run the business on my own – pretty heavy blackmail! I had so little self-confidence that I didn't believe I could do it on my own so I gave in and she became a director.

Four years later, my second son died at the age of twenty-six. This nearly annihilated me. I made an absolute commitment to myself that he hadn't died in vain – that I'd stop being a wimp and make him proud of me. I left my husband, started my own business and I'm now running a very successful business doing what I'm passionate about. I make more profit each year than in the entire time I was in business with my last husband. If I'd seen the first problem as an opportunity, taken my courage in both hands and left, then I wouldn't have suffered another four years of unhappiness and I'd still have had some money left. Moreover, if I'd left when the problem first arose and my son had been able to move with me into different circumstances, he may have been alive today.

YOUR CHOICE

It's up to you how you view each situation that you find yourself in. I actually believe that there's no such thing as coincidence and that everything happens for a reason, so in any real difficulty I invariably ask myself, 'If I knew that what is happening right now is exactly as it's meant to be, how might I now view it and what might I now do?' That question practically forces me into viewing the situation as an opportunity.

Christopher Reeve faced a problem that most people just couldn't imagine – an accident that left him totally paralysed. He was an inspiration to millions because he turned such a ghastly situation into an opportunity. Michael J. Fox, the actor who has contracted Parkinson's disease, is another inspiration. In his book, he actually says that the experience has changed him for the better and that he's learned so much from it. I come across many people who have been made redundant, some of them late enough in life to think that getting another job is going to be really difficult. I've see them deal with this in totally different ways, from thinking their life is over through to 'Wow, this is great, I can now find a way to do the things that I've always wanted to.' The latter 'can do' attitude is powerful – it brings opportunities and possibilities, it opens our hearts and minds to new experiences and life becomes a joy rather than something to be endured.

IDEA 36, *Learning from mistakes*, provides further insights into turning problems around.

Try another idea...

'When one door opens, another one closes – but we often look so long and so regretfully upon the closed door that we do not see the one that has opened for us.'
ALEXANDER GRAHAM BELL

Defining idea...

How did it go?

Q   **My daughter is determined to leave school this year, without A levels. She's exceptionally bright, but I can't convince her that she's likely to struggle because so many jobs won't be available to her. How do I persuade her to rethink?**

A   *It seems that while you're viewing the situation as a problem, your daughter sees it as an opportunity. You have the assumption that she won't do well without qualifications. She has the assumption that she will. First ask yourself the question I described earlier. More importantly, back off and spend time simply listening to your daughter and supporting her thinking. The more you push her, the more she's likely to resist. Encourage her to think for herself – I'm sure she'll be more than capable of making her own decisions. I now run my own business, yet I left school with no qualifications!*

Q   **My boss panics at the slightest thing and turns little problems into big ones. The office is in a permanent state of crisis, which is partly why we've recently lost two of our best people. How can I get him to see that his reaction to problems makes things worse?**

A   *I believe that every individual wants to be the best they can be, so I suggest you tell your boss what you've told me. He won't be able to give you his undivided attention in such a chaotic atmosphere so take him out for a drink and try to establish why he feels the need to behave in this way. Explain the outcome of his current behaviour and also the likely outcome if he were to behave differently. Offer to help him find more constructive ways to do things and ask how you can support him in making the required changes.*

49

Involve them all

Some people are quieter than others at meetings. They might be nervous about sharing their ideas, and we need to find a way to help them.

How many meetings have you attended where the loudest voices get their ideas across and others are left frustrated because they feel they're not listened to and consequently not valued?

WHO HAS THE BEST IDEAS?

When you have a discussion group at work or home it's valuable to get ideas from everyone. There's absolutely no point in having someone at a meeting who doesn't open their mouth. Apart from anything else, it's a serious waste of money if it's a work meeting. If an individual has nothing to contribute then there's no point in them wasting their time and yours. What usually happens at meetings, unless communicating behaviours are well and truly learned and practised, is that those with the loudest voices and the most seniority get their ideas heard and driven through.

Here's an idea for you...

At your next group discussion make a note of who's doing the most talking and who's really not contributing. Ask yourself why you wish to have the latter at this meeting and what value you'd like them to bring. If they're there just for the sake of it, then they could be doing something better with their time. If, however, you believe they do have something to contribute, then put your plan together. Before the next meeting decide on the questions you can ask them that won't threaten and intimidate them but instead help them feel that they've something to offer. Now build on that.

Unfortunately, what can then happen is that people who feel they haven't been heard begin to wreck the idea subversively. Not necessarily intentionally, but because they feel uncomfortable with the decision they begin to talk to other people about their concerns. People might begin to listen to these concerns, understand them and perhaps have some agreement with them. This will then de-motivate them from doing the job in the way that's been agreed and there will be a significant dilution of the agreed actions. This in turn can lead to real frustration at the next meeting, with the boss shouting 'But we agreed that this is what we were going to do!' All of this because someone who may be quiet or nervous in coming forward feels unfairly treated because they haven't been listened to. Do we have the right to assume that quiet people don't have great ideas? Maybe they have the balance the right way round – it's called two ears and one mouth!

A CONSIDERED APPROACH

We need to learn how to involve each person and encourage their contribution. If someone is shy or nervous, asking them to give an opinion in a situation where they might feel exposed and threatened is likely to have the opposite impact to the one you're after. If you get it wrong, they'll probably become even more nervous. Consequently, they won't be able to think well and their ideas aren't likely to be as good. All this can lead to them thinking they have no value, and the downward spiral continues.

I suggest that you ask the first question in this way: 'Carol, that opportunity that we were talking about in your office the other day, I think it was excellent and that it would be extremely useful if you could share that with the group at this point.' What you've done is tell Carol that her idea is a good one, that you think it has value and that you're supporting her. She'll now share her idea with the group, after which you make a point of thanking her. You've now shown her that talking in the group need not be a scary experience. You may now need to do something similar at the next two or three meetings. After this, she'll hopefully begin to have the courage to come to the meeting and add real value knowing that she has something to contribute.

You may wish to consider how you can extend people's ideas to begin to create real synergy and teamwork. Look at IDEA 15, *Whose idea is it anyway?*

Try another idea...

'There is no stimulus like that which comes from the consciousness of knowing that others believe in us.'
ORISON SWEET MARDEN, US editor and motivational writer

Defining idea...

217

Q **I've a large team and I'd never realised how quiet a couple of people in the team are. One of them is the only woman in the entire team – should I handle her any differently?**

A   *Why, in a large team, do you only have one woman? What a missed opportunity! Anyway, the simple answer is 'no'. Why would she want to be treated any differently than her male colleagues? You just need to be sure that you don't overdo the support, as you don't want her colleagues to start thinking that she's getting favoured. It would probably be wise to invite contributions in a similar way from a couple of the others as well.*

Q **I have five children and one of them is really quiet. It's difficult to extract any ideas from her at all. How can I deal with this?**

A   *If she's that quiet I'd see if I could dig a little deeper to see what might be going on. Is there something upsetting her and causing this quietness? However, I'd still want her to feel that her ideas are valued by the family, for the more she can learn that she has value in a group, the easier it's likely to be for her in later life. How about seeing if you can coax some ideas from her when she's on her own with you and then you can share them with the rest of the family when you're all together? This might inspire her to start to share them herself. When she does, be sure to give her lots of support and encouragement, and make sure that the rest of the family don't interrupt her or drown her out.*

50

So where am I at?

Trying to do everything at once can create a feeling of being overwhelmed. The ability to focus on the key things can help you truly begin to transform your life.

What are the key messages that we might take away from exploring the many different thoughts about how we can view the world and ourselves differently?

TOO MUCH INFORMATION

When I started on my path of growth, I never stopped reading – at least a book a week. I went on countless workshops and was becoming a personal growth junkie! There was so much to learn and I ended up being confused by so much information. I was trying to change all of me at once and, guess what, feeling I wasn't good enough yet again. So, after much heartache I realised that what I needed to do was simplify everything that I'd learned. The more I studied the clearer it became that the key to everything was responsibility: where I was in my life was because of the decisions that I'd made. If I was in an abusive relationship that was because I'd chosen to go into it and was also choosing to stay in it; if I was unhappy it was because that was the way I was choosing to feel; if I was at

Here's an idea for you... **Find a quiet place to think about all the new ideas that could transform your life. Which is the one that keeps floating back into your mind? Which resonated the most with some aspect of your life? Now commit to that one idea for a month and forget all the others. Stay with it until you feel it's internalised and only then build on it with another idea. Also, read anything and everything that expands your knowledge and understanding of personal development. I think that everyone should read *Time to Think* by Nancy Kline.**

loggerheads with one of my children that was because I was choosing not to sort it out; and so on. It was definitely the toughest thing of all for me to face up to and deal with, but each time I made myself come back to the simplicity of this message the more everything slotted into place. It helped me to stay focused in the present moment, it helped me to become aware of how I communicated in each moment and it helped me challenge the way I was thinking on a daily basis.

WHEN I'M DOWN, I'M DOWN!

It's so easy for us to get very depressed and feel that we can never get out of that dark place. I remember when one of my clients told me that she used to suffer from depression – not clinical depression. She'd been prescribed antidepressants for years and they were now stronger than ever. She felt that she was never going to improve. She actually described herself as someone with depression, which had become part of who she was. The first thing I did was to get her to distance herself from the problem rather than *be* the problem, to think of herself as someone who chooses depressive thoughts. She found this really challenging at first and used to phone me and say things like, 'My boss has just been ghastly to me and because of that I feel terrible, it's her fault but I can't help it.' I persuaded her that if she really felt she couldn't change how she felt, to consciously choose it. To tell everyone around her that today she was choosing to be depressed and to stay away from her. She was going to wallow in misery and enjoy every bit of it! By lunchtime she'd had enough and began to recognise that she could choose to feel different. Bit by bit she began to own and take responsibility for how she felt and to change it. She's now been off antidepressants for five years.

Refresh your thinking about where we really do have control – see IDEA 1, *Who you are is what you get.*

Try another idea...

Another part of this story that I found fascinating is that when she went to see the doctor to ask if she could begin to reduce her intake of antidepressants, the doctor's response was, 'No, I don't think that would be a good idea.' In my opinion, the doctor was actively discouraging her from taking responsibility for her own health and wellbeing!

'The highest reward for a person's toil is not what they get for it, but what they become by it.'
JOHN RUSKIN

Defining idea...

221

How did it go?

Q   I was really pleased to read this idea because I was trying to do too much at once and becoming confused. But if I do what you suggest here, isn't there a chance that I could end up staying with just one idea?

A   *It depends which idea you choose. If it's doing your vision and working towards that, then possibly. If it's about responsibility, no, because that links into everything. It's your choice. Decide on your vision and what you want to change, and then plan how you can do that and keep moving forward. You either take 100% responsibility for your own development or you don't.*

Q   You make it sound so simple, but I think it's really difficult. How long did it take you to get to where you are right now?

A   *A masterful question! I know I make it sound easy, and if you read and understand the small steps that are required to transform your life, it probably is easy. What I'm suggesting isn't rocket science, it's common sense and you probably already know it all. I'm just bringing it back to your conscious awareness. It took me forever! I've been doing this for ten years now and I'm still learning and I still slip regularly. The best advice I can give you is to teach it as I do. I consequently keep reminding myself of things that I know and still forget. I don't necessarily mean formally, but at any opportunity you get with your children, colleagues and friends. Think of a way to share these insights, and make it fun. Keep asking for feedback on how you're doing and keep practising. Oh, and don't forget to keep telling yourself how well you're doing!*

51
Living in the moment

Far too much time is spent worrying about the future or the mistakes that we've made in the past.

We have no power over the past as we can't change it, and we can't control the future. We only have power in the present moment, and this is where we can make change happen.

THE PRESENT

Many years ago I read a book called *The Present* that affected me profoundly. I read it many times over. The simplicity of the message is profound: it's only in each individual moment that we can make changes – the moment that we're living in right now. I know that I used to spend so much of my time looking backwards, worrying about something that had happened or something that I'd said or done and thinking about how I could have done it differently. I can't begin to imagine how much of my life I've wasted looking backwards and trying to change the unchangeable. On top of that, I've wished away time planning what I'm going to do

Here's an idea for you...

Spend the next hour thinking only about the present. Become aware of what you're doing in each moment. Appreciate each moment and become aware of everything in and around you – every movement you make, how your body feels, each sound around you. See how much you can notice while you're doing whatever it is you're doing. Become aware of your breathing and how you're feeling. You may even choose to ask, 'What could I do in this moment, right now, that may improve my life or the life of someone I care about?' The following day you could increase the hour to two hours, then continue to build on this until you start to really live your life in the present moment.

or say in the future. I kept forgetting that I only have the power to make change in the here and now – in the present. What can I do right now that may change today, this relationship or open a new opportunity? What can I do right now that could help my children feel better about themselves, make the world a better place or allow my colleagues to think better for themselves?

HAPPINESS IS A CHOICE

When I look at each moment as I'm living it, there's nothing that I can't cope with. That has to be a truth otherwise I wouldn't be here. So, why did I continually worry about how I would cope in the future? In the present moment, there's always something that I can do and

that's what we so easily forget. Nearly always, the times when I'm feeling unhappy are when I'm thinking about something that's already happened or worrying about something that might happen. Yet, if I truly focus on where I am right now, on the present, I can choose to be happy irrespective of what I'm doing, whether I'm cleaning the house, doing the ironing or writing this book.

Look back at your vision and see if you want to add anything to it. If you haven't yet done your vision, now might be a good time. Try IDEA 24, *Why plan your life?*

Try another idea...

'Present-moment living, getting in touch with your now, is at the heart of effective living. When you think about it, there really is no other moment you can live. Now is all there is, and the future is just another present moment to live when it arrives.'
WAYNE DYER, author and self-help expert

Defining idea...

How did it go? **Q** **I can't believe how difficult it is to live in the present. I had no idea how much I lived in the past and the future. Does it become any easier?**

A *This is something that I still find challenging. It was a real shock to me too but it does become easier. The challenge is remembering to do it, so find a way to remind yourself daily. Even if you only do a few minutes each day you'll notice a difference in the way you live your life and become more conscious in each moment. It's like going to the gym or taking exercise – firstly raising your level of awareness, then following with commitment and determination to the point where it becomes second nature.*

Q **Doesn't this conflict with creating a vision for your life where you have to think about the future?**

A *I understand where you're coming from and how it can sound like these are two conflicting ideas, but I actually think that the opposite is the case. Doing a vision and thinking about how you want your life to be is wonderful. However, thinking about it all the time probably isn't helpful because you're giving away the power of the present moment. Remember that it's only in the here and now that we can do something that will lead us towards achieving our vision. Create your vision, let go of the outcome and then do whatever it takes in the present to move you towards where you want to be.*

Keeping it going

I hope that you've adopted some new ideas and have a fresh vision for your life. You can now continue along the exciting path of developing yourself to achieve everything you wish for.

When the first exciting phase of a project has passed, it's sometimes difficult to stay committed and enthusiastic. How do you maintain your progress towards your new vision?

KEEP REMINDING YOURSELF OF WHAT'S IMPORTANT TO YOU

Isn't it strange how when we commit to doing something for other people, whether at work or at home, we can remain totally focused on delivering for them? Our professionalism at work and our love at home drive us to keep our promises. However, when we're doing something solely for ourselves, we often lose interest for some reason. We start to make excuses. We might miss one of the classes where we were learning an essential skill we need to help us achieve our goal. We allow other events and 'priorities' to waylay us. There are a number of things that help me to stay focused on what's important to me.

Here's an
idea for
you...

Share your vision with your family and friends so that they understand why you're taking on new challenges and acting in different ways. They are then much more likely to support you and help keep you focused on your dream. Of course it's also important to encourage them to create their own vision. Remember to support all of their dreams, no matter how you feel about them. This is their vision for their life!

Write down your goals, being very clear and specific about exactly what they are. What will it be like when you've achieved them? What will it look like, feel like, and so on? Then keep them in view so that you see them every day. I keep mine in my diary; other people put them in their knicker drawer or in their in-trays. I've even known one person who made his vision his screensaver! I also keep my values written in my diary so that I see them every day too and this helps me when I have difficult decisions to make.

Constantly seeing my vision means that it's never far from my thoughts and I find that I keep asking myself, 'What could I do today to move a step closer to achieving my vision?'

FIND A BUDDY

Another way is to find someone to be your coaching 'buddy'. This is something that many people have found useful. Share your ideas and your vision with someone else. You might also like to help them develop their own vision. Then you can work together to encourage and inspire each other. Revisit your plans and share your progress. If you feel that there are blocks in the way of either of you achieving your goals, use incisive questions to break through the block.

I encourage people who come on my programmes to use the buddy system. They pair up, exchange numbers and speak to each other on a regular basis for a few months to provide support whilst they're gradually putting their action plans into place. I'm still in touch with some of the delegates from my very first programmes and after nearly nine years they're still in touch with their buddies! It really works.

Whether it's a buddy or continuous reminders in the home or at work, you need a system in place to keep you driving towards your personal goals.

IDEA 24, *Why plan your life?*, looks at another angle in respect of achieving your vision.

Try another idea...

'Success is focusing the full power of all you are on what you have a burning desire to achieve.'
WILFRED PETERSON

Defining idea...

How did it go?

Q I found a buddy to work with. She's a really good friend of mine. However, when I encouraged her to create her own vision I found out that she really wants to go and live in France within the next couple of years. I'm devastated because I'll miss her so much. How can I now support her to live her dream?

A *I can understand how you feel, but this is about helping someone you love to fulfil their potential and their dreams. If you provide all the support that she needs to achieve her goal then you'll feel rewarded anyway. Focus on what you can give and let go of the outcome. Real friendship like your friendship will stand the test, and I'm sure you'll spend many happy times together in both France and at home.*

Q I really want to create changes in my life, but I don't know whether I can actually go through with them. I know that I'm not completely fulfilled right now, but is the grass really greener? And what if I achieve my dream and discover that it's not what I want after all?

A *Along the path to achieving your vision there will probably be times when you want to make adjustments. Nothing is cast in stone. What have you got to lose? You may find that you create a new dream as soon as you reach your current goal, but you'll have learned a great deal along the way and no doubt you'll be nearer to the new goal than you are today. In my experience we rarely regret the things we do, but we almost always regret what we don't do. Don't give up on your dream!*

The end...

Or is it a new beginning?

We hope that the ideas in this book will have inspired you to try some new things. You should be well on your way to a more fulfilled, creative, inspired you, brimming with ideas and ambition.

You're mean, you're motivated and you don't care who knows it.

So why not let us know all about it? Tell us how you got on. What did it for you – what helped you beat the demons that were holding you back? Maybe you've got some tips of your own you want to share (see next page if so). And if you liked this book you may find we have even more brilliant ideas that could change other areas of your life for the better.

You'll find the Infinite Ideas crew waiting for you online at www.infideas.com.

Or if you prefer to write, then send your letters to:
Transform your life
The Infinite Ideas Company Ltd
Belsyre Court, 57 Woodstock Road, Oxford OX2 6JH, United Kingdom

We want to know what you think, because we're all working on making our lives better too. Give us your feedback and you could win a copy of another *52 Brilliant Ideas* book of your choice. Or maybe get a crack at writing your own.

Good luck. Be brilliant.

Offer one

CASH IN YOUR IDEAS

We hope you enjoy this book. We hope it inspires, amuses, educates and entertains you. But we don't assume that you're a novice, or that this is the first book that you've bought on the subject. You've got ideas of your own. Maybe our author has missed an idea that you use successfully. If so, why not send it to info@infideas.com, and if we like it we'll post it on our bulletin board. Better still, if your idea makes it into print we'll send you £50 and you'll be fully credited so that everyone knows you've had another Brilliant Idea.

Offer two

HOW COULD YOU REFUSE?

Amazing discounts on bulk quantities of Infinite Ideas books are available to corporations, professional associations and other organizations.

For details call us on:
+44 (0)1865 292045
fax: +44 (0)1865 292001
or e-mail: info@infideas.com

Acknowledgements

There are so many people that I would like to acknowledge that it is hard to know where to begin. Firstly, without Philip Blackwell telling me that my book needed to be written and then introducing me to Richard Burton I wouldn't be writing this at all, so a big thank you for challenging me and then especially to Richard for encouraging and supporting me. Ken, I know the agonies you went through in trying to get into my head so you could help me write this and I couldn't have done it without you. I am just sorry my head proved so challenging! There are many wonderful personal development 'gurus' out there and there are three who profoundly affected me. Wayne Dyer and Patch Adams in different ways are memorable for me. Nancy Kline is one of the world's special people and much of my work is based on her teachings. Thank you Nancy for being an inspiration, a wonderful coach and teacher, and just for being you.

There are so many clients, colleagues and friends who have been my inspiration and my teachers – too numerous to name all of them. Every person that I have worked with, coached and trained has added to my development and growth in some way. Without you stretching me to explore my own thinking I would not be where I am today. One or two I would like to name. Scott Davidson, who had enough faith in me to ask this totally unqualified lady to be his coach, challenged me to 'go it alone', to believe in myself and not feel the need to join a bigger company. His sudden, tragic death has left a gap in my life which will always remain. Michael O'Byrne – what courage to take my work into the police. You always were a maverick and I will treasure the words you said to me at my sixtieth-birthday celebrations.

All of my friends and colleagues inspire me and never cease to amaze me, you are all special people. Jim and Kirsten, you are a living, breathing example of what we teach and the impact you have on so many lives is awesome. Christine, without you this book would never have reached fruition, you gave of yourself until you nearly collapsed – I owe you one! You are the greatest support and the most loving and valued friend. Sherilyn, you only came into my life recently and I hope you never leave it – bringing you into my business is the best thing I ever did. As a colleague and as a friend you have impacted me more than you know. Bruce and Hazel, what would I have done without you? Hazel – what can I say? My very best friend for twenty-six years. You have always been there for me, through the hell and the fun times. You have only supported and encouraged me and never complained! My life is the richer for having you in it. So many wonderful people. If I listed you all it would be pages long but I hope you all know how much I appreciate each and every one of you.

I guess that I cannot complete this list without a big 'thank you' to my three ex-husbands. Without those experiences I may not be where I am today. I especially am pleased that Bob became a good friend and am very sad that he missed this book by weeks. Mike too, and I hope you cope with the references to you and I thank you too for your great speech at my sixtieth.

And so to my family – extended, past and present! You have all been great and I am sure one day I will write memories about all of you, especially Dad. James, Richard, Lucy, Emma and Mark, my lovely children. It is thanks to you that I found the courage to drag myself out of the mire and carry on when things were at their toughest. It is wonderful to see so many of you settled and happy and I thank you for being the wonderful human beings that you are. Leslie, thank you for coming back into my life and being the special man that you are. I hope you will always be there to love, encourage and support me.

Finally, I dedicate every page of this book to my beloved Phil. You may have only lived for twenty-six years but you taught me so much. You were the most special son and I feel honoured to have been your mother. Without you I would not have had the courage to turn my life around. I pray that the catalytic event of your death has enabled me to positively impact many other lives. It is all thanks to you, my darling boy.

Where it's at...

acknowledge good ideas, 63
action plan, 86, 115
adult cynicism, 132
Angelou, Maya, 115, 145
Apollinaire, Guillaume, 33
appreciated, 13-14, 33, 132
appreciation, 2, 3, 13, 15-17, 51-52, 69, 76
Ashe, Arthur, 3
asking questions to test our understanding, 123
assumptions, 15, 19, 21, 29, 55-56, 77, 79-80, 83,
    98, 153-154, 158

Bach, Richard, 159
beliefs, 29, 77, 82, 91, 93, 117, 154, 161, 163,
    164, 186, 187, 189
    changing beliefs, 27
changing beliefs, 27
Bell, Alexander Graham, 213
Brown, Rita Mae, 47

coaching buddy, 229, 230
Campbell, Joseph, 87
questions, carefully chosen, 81
Carnegie, Dale, 15
children, 2-4, 8, 14-16, 29, 30, 39-40, 42, 44, 48,
    51, 57, 68, 73-74, 78, 92-93, 96, 101, 104,
    106, 109, 116-118, 120, 127, 131-134, 136,
    141, 145, 149, 150, 165-166, 168, 178,
    179-180, 184-185, 198-199, 201-202, 204,
    207, 218, 220, 222, 224
choices about how we live, 85

choose to be happy, 175-176, 225
communication, 9, 64, 81, 121, 185, 195
communication skills, 9
conditioning, 132-133, 187-190
confidence, 31-34, 84, 93, 98, 104, 182, 212
    lack of, 31, 32
Cossman, E. Joseph, 155
Cousins, Park, 189
Covey, Stephen, 144
Covey, Steven, 207
creative ideas, 143, 169

de la Rochefoucald, François, 127
decisions, 10, 12, 43, 45, 67, 93, 96, 111, 113,
    124, 144, 149, 158, 162-163, 189, 201, 214,
    219, 228
    making for yourself, 45
developing yourself, 227
development activities, 135-136
Dewey, John, 29
disagreeing, 109, 119, 169-170, 205
disempowering words, 46, 48
diversity of views, 143
dream, 60, 105-106, 228, 230
Dyer, Wayne, 137, 181, 225

each day as a blessing, 180
Eaton, Bob, 185
emotions, driven by, 70, 110, 111, 134, 175
encouragement, 2, 49, 56, 58, 63-64, 73, 110-111,
    127, 148, 150, 204

exercises, 96, 98, 197
expectations, 95, 162

family, 2, 10, 27, 29, 37–38, 40–42, 44, 56, 59, 80, 85, 87, 98, 106, 118–119, 121, 142, 144, 149, 158, 170, 181, 185, 218, 228
feedback, 8, 14, 43, 66, 116–118, 120, 159, 196, 199, 222, 232
feelings, 5, 34, 109, 111, 144–145, 159, 160, 170, 206
first impressions, 19
focusing on the key things, 219
Fox, Michael J., 213
fresh vision, 227
fury, 109–111
future, worrying about the, 223

Gandhi, Mahatma, 203
great leader, 8, 59, 75
Greenleaf, Robert, 3
group exercise, 1
group introductions, 21
Guinon, Albert, 149

happiness, 22, 26, 44, 59, 92, 104, 112, 120, 162, 164, 167, 175, 176–178, 181, 225, 230
hear ideas in our own words, 113

ideas, hearing in our own words, 113
Heinlein, Robert A., 141
helping others to think things through, 67
Hemingway, Ernest, 69
Heraclitus, 123
hierarchy, 147
Holden, Robert, 175
holding you back, 28, 154, 164

Holmes, Oliver Wendell, 105
Hubbard, Elbert, 21
imagination, 131, 132, 134, 154
incisive questions, 77–80, 83, 114–116, 126, 128, 154, 229
influencing people, 57, 99, 127, 193, 195

Jong, Erica, 83
Joubert, Joseph, 171

key things, focusing on, 219
Kline, Nancy, 68, 79, 220

lack of confidence, 31, 32
language, 45–46, 48, 100, 102, 113–114, 122
   changing, 46
Lao Tzu, 199
leaders, 7, 8, 22, 37, 38, 59, 75, 117–119, 147, 150, 183, 185–186, 188, 196
leadership, 3, 9, 22, 37–39, 62, 67, 150, 183, 186, 207
leadership style, 37
learning from our mistakes, 157
liberating your thinking, 15, 29, 77, 79, 83, 115, 155

mistakes, learning from our, 157
thinking, liberating your, 15, 29, 77, 79, 83, 115, 155
Lincoln, Abraham, 177
listen and influence, 101
listening, 2, 4, 9–10, 12, 57, 63, 68–70, 81, 99, 102, 111–112, 113, 115, 121, 124–127, 133, 144, 146–147, 149, 170, 196–197, 205–207, 214
listening partner, 115, 126

loudest voices, 215
love, 14, 16, 24, 26, 80, 88, 91, 106, 136, 146, 156, 165–168, 176, 180, 199, 227, 230

maintenance activities, 135–136
making decisions for yourself, 45
Marden, Orison Sweet, 217
Marshall, John, 195
Maslow, Abraham, 61
McGregor, Douglas, 55, 56
mistakes, 15, 42, 120, 154, 157, 159–160, 198, 213, 223
Mizner, Wilson, 101
moment of choice, 25, 30, 139, 141
motivation, 2, 49, 50–51, 55, 73, 75, 118, 137
motivation to change, 73
Muller, Robert, 7
Nance, Revd W. A., 75
needs in life, 59
new beginning, 179
no power over the past, 223

obituary, writing your own, 96, 197-200
one person, being, 5, 6, 8, 21, 125, 153, 228
open our minds, 144
own my life, 95, 96, 97
ownership of an idea, 149

partner, 3, 14, 26, 70, 70, 86, 92, 100–101, 106, 112, 115, 126, 136, 138, 140–141, 162, 166–168, 172, 198, 207
personal development, 6, 79, 181, 220
Peter, Laurence J., 111
Peters, Tom, 51
Peterson, Wilfred, 229
Picasso, Pablo, 133

plan your life, 33, 103, 105, 107, 153, 163, 225, 229
positive mental attitude, 23
positive philosophy, 155
power in the present moment, 223

rank, 147, 148
Reeve, Christopher, 200, 213
relationship, 3, 20, 30, 59, 78, 92, 93, 94, 97, 100, 110, 114, 116, 120, 135–138, 146, 166, 167, 178, 211, 219, 224
relationships, 9, 21, 49, 51, 100, 104, 121, 137, 138–139, 141
repeating useless patterns, 27
resolving issues, 205, 207
responsibility, 1, 4, 25, 30, 50, 56–58, 75, 93, 119, 139, 141, 146, 150, 157, 166, 168, 184–186, 204, 219, 221–222
Roddick, Anita, 57
Roosevelt, Eleanor, 93
Ruskin, John, 221
Ruth, Babe, 43

say 'no', idea 46,
saying 'no',
Seneca, 97
sense of achievement, 74
servant leadership, 3
share our ideas, 63, 144
Steinbeck, John, 65
strengths, 6, 14–15, 42–43, 117, 124, 146
successful salespeople, 99
supporting, 2, 3, 56, 74, 100, 179, 196, 207, 214, 217
Swetchine, Anne-Sophie, 167
systems of recognition, 74

take full responsibility, 1
teamwork, 41, 43, 63, 65, 217
Theory X, management style, 55–58
Theory Y, management style, 55–57
think creatively, 81
think like giants, 51, 131, 133
thinking partnerships, 125
thinking session, 82, 149
thinking things through, helping others to, 67
trainers, 7, 33
trust, 4, 56–58, 118–120, 198
turn them into opportunities, problems, 211
two people, are you?, 5–8, 65

victim, 93, 153
vision, 4, 31, 33, 42–44, 78–79, 103–106,
    137–138, 146, 148, 156, 163–164, 183, 222,
    225, 226–230

Waitley, Denis, 25
Washington, Martha, 181
work–life balance, 86–87, 203
workshops, 6, 31, 33, 93, 137, 219
worrying about the future, 223